The Lamentations of Jeremiah

BIBLE STUDY GUIDE

From the Bible-teaching ministry of

Charles R. Swindoll

INSIGHT FOR LIVING

These studies are based on the outlines of sermons delivered by Charles R. Swindoll. Chuck is a graduate of Dallas Theological Seminary and has served in pastorates for over twenty-three years, including churches in Texas, New England, and California. Since 1971 he has served as senior pastor of the First Evangelical Free Church of Fullerton, California. Chuck's radio program, "Insight for Living," began in 1979. In addition to his church and radio ministries, Chuck has authored twenty books and numerous booklets on a variety of subjects.

Chuck's outlines are expanded from the sermon transcripts and the text is coauthored by Bill Watkins, a graduate of California State University at Fresno and Dallas Theological Seminary. The Living Insights are written by Bill Butterworth, a graduate of Florida Bible College, Dallas Theological Seminary, and Florida Atlantic University. Bill Watkins is presently the director of educational resources, and Bill Butterworth is currently the director of counseling ministries at Insight for Living.

Editor in Chief:	Cynthia Swindoll
Coauthor of Text:	Bill Watkins
Author of Living Insights:	Bill Butterworth
Copy Supervisor:	Wendy Jones
Editorial Assistants:	Glenda Gardner, Jane Gillis, and Julie Martin
Director, Communications Division:	Carla Beck
Project Supervisor:	Nina Paris
Art Director:	Ed Kesterson
Production Artist:	Donna Mayo
Typographers:	Bob Haskins and Debbie Krumland
Calligrapher:	Richard Stumpf
Cover:	The Wailing Wall, Israel; photograph by Gordon Gahan/Photo Researchers, Inc.
Production Supervisor:	Deedee Snyder
Printer:	Frye and Smith

ISBN 0-8499-8284-7

Ordering Information

An album that contains eight messages on four cassettes and corresponds to this study guide may be purchased through Insight for Living, Post Office Box 4444, Fullerton, California 92634. For ordering information and a current catalog, please write our offices or call (714) 870-9161.

Canadian residents may obtain a catalog and ordering information through Insight for Living Ministries, Post Office Box 2510, Vancouver, British Columbia, Canada V6B 3W7, (604) 272-5811. Overseas residents should direct their correspondence to our Fullerton office.

If you wish to order by Visa or MasterCard, you are welcome to use our toll-free number, (800) 772-8888, Monday through Friday between the hours of 8:30 A.M. and 4:00 P.M., Pacific time. This number may be used anywhere in the continental United States excluding Alaska, California, and Hawaii. Orders from those areas can be made by calling our general office number, (714) 870-9161.

Table of Contents

The Lamentations of Jeremiah

Reaping what we sow is a principle as old as Scripture. Time and again we see examples of it in the Bible, as well as in life all around us. Theoretically, we know it is true, and experientially, we have witnessed it, but we tend to forget.

Prisons exist, standing as stern evidence that crime does not pay. Both drug rehabilitation centers and special clinics for alcoholics are reminders that our bodies cannot be mistreated without severe consequences. Again, the reminder—we reap what we sow.

There is a small book hidden in the folds of the Old Testament that many people have never stopped to read. It is a mute reminder that sin, in spite of all its allurement and excitement, carries with it the heavy weights of sorrow, grief, misery, barrenness, and pain. It is the other side of the "eat, drink, and be merry" coin. It is Lamentations, *Jeremiah's grim, bold announcement that a holy God will not remain silent forever when His people disobey Him.*

This is a serious yet timely series for a day when reaping what we sow is an unpopular message. May all of us hear and take heed. The prophet Jeremiah speaks truth we dare not ignore.

Chuck Swindoll

Putting Truth into Action

Knowledge apart from application falls short of God's desire for His children. Knowledge must result in change and growth. Consequently, we have constructed this Bible study guide with these purposes in mind: (1) to stimulate discovery, (2) to increase understanding, and (3) to encourage application.

At the end of each lesson is a section called 🖼️ ***Living Insights.** There you'll be given assistance in further Bible study, thoughtful interaction, and personal appropriation. This is the place where the lesson is fitted with shoe leather for your walk through the varied experiences of life.*

It's our hope that you'll discover numerous ways to use this tool. Some useful avenues we would suggest are personal meditation, joint discovery, and discussion with your spouse, family, work associates, friends, or neighbors. The study guide is also practical for church classes and, of course, as a study aid for the "Insight for Living" radio broadcast. The individual studies can usually be completed in thirty minutes. However, some are more open-ended and could be expanded for greater depth. Their use is flexible!

In order to derive the greatest benefit from this process, we suggest that you record your responses to the lessons in a notebook where writing space is plentiful. In view of the kinds of questions asked, your notebook may become a journal filled with your many discoveries and commitments. We anticipate that you will find yourself returning to it periodically for review and encouragement.

Bill Watkins
Coauthor of Text

Bill Butterworth
Author of Living Insights

The Lamentations of Jeremiah

The Prophet Who Cried a Lot
Jeremiah 1:1–10, 16–19

"It's not manly to cry." How often these words have come from the lips of well-intentioned people! Thinking that tears are a sign of either weakness or a lack of faith in God, people have squelched expressions of sorrow and hurt in both themselves and others. But the Lord does not look at crying in the same way many of us may. In Psalm 56:8, we learn that He remembers and preserves our tears. And in the Gospel of John we read about the Son of God weeping bitterly while standing before the tomb of Lazarus (John 11:34–35). To many who witnessed this event, His sobs were viewed as a display of His great love for a close friend (v. 36). Throughout Scripture we find that the people of God openly expressed their pain to one another as well as to the Lord (see 1 Sam. 20:40–41, 2 Sam. 13:34–36). One prophet even recorded his sorrow in a book known today as Lamentations. This composition of Jeremiah's—a divinely inspired record of human pain—will be our focus in the lessons to follow. But before we turn our attention to this book, let's gain an understanding of Jeremiah—the man, his times, and his ministry. Much of this information can be found in the first chapter of the Book of Jeremiah.

I. Jeremiah and His Times
Jeremiah 1:1–3 tells us the following about the prophet of lament:

> The words of Jeremiah, the son of Hilkiah, of the priests who were in Anathoth in the land of Benjamin, to whom the word of the Lord came in the days of Josiah, the son of Amon, king of Judah, in the thirteenth year of his reign. It came also in the days of Jehoiakim, the son of Josiah, king of Judah, until the end of the eleventh year of Zedekiah, the son of Josiah, king of Judah, until the exile of Jerusalem in the fifth month.

Let's examine these verses more closely.

A. His name. The exact meaning of the name *Jeremiah* is disputed, but many Bible scholars understand it to mean "the

1

Lord throws."[1] In light of this and the ministry he was given, it becomes clear that Jeremiah did not fit the mold of a successful prophet of God; he was tossed into his times by the Lord to deliver an unwelcome message to the Jewish people.

B. His roots. Jeremiah's birthplace was Anathoth, a little village that was located about three miles northeast of Jerusalem. Hilkiah was the name of his father. Hilkiah may have been a descendant of the priest Abiathar, who was himself banished to Anathoth by King Solomon (1 Kings 2:26). Some early commentators and historians, such as Jerome, identify Jeremiah's father as the high priest who discovered " 'the book of the [Mosaic] law' " during Josiah's reign in 622 B.C. (2 Kings 22:8).[2] Whether this identification is correct or not is uncertain. But one fact is clear: Hilkiah was a priest who lived among other priests in Anathoth. This indicates that Jeremiah was destined for the priesthood ... until the Lord intervened.

C. His world. In order to understand Jeremiah's times, we must step back several years in Israel's history. During the reigns of Saul, David, and Solomon, the nation of Israel became a strong political unit. However, after the death of King Solomon in 931 B.C., Israel experienced a civil war that divided it into two nations—the northern kingdom, which retained the name Israel, and the southern kingdom, which was called Judah. This national cleavage, coupled with religious corruption and politico-economic instability, eventually led to the demise of both kingdoms. Israel continued as a nation for just over two centuries. During that time, she had nineteen kings, eight of whom either committed suicide or were assassinated. God considered none of her rulers to be good because each permitted or promoted the worship of false deities. Finally, in 722 B.C., the Assyrian ruler Shalmaneser V conquered Israel and took 27,290 Jews captive to Mesopotamia and Media (see 2 Kings 17:1–18), "where they vanished from history."[3] Judah, on the other hand, lasted as a nation for 345 years, approximately one and a half centuries longer than Israel. Twenty kings governed Judah, and eight of them followed God's ways. Under her rulers there

1. See Gleason L. Archer, Jr., *A Survey of Old Testament Introduction*, rev. ed. (Chicago: Moody Press, 1974), p. 359; Sven K. Soderlund, "Jeremiah," in *The International Standard Bible Encyclopedia*, 4 vols., rev. ed. (Grand Rapids, Mich.: William B. Eerdmans Publishing Co., 1979, 1982, 1986), vol. 2, p. 984.

2. See Sven K. Soderlund, "Jeremiah, Book of," in *The International Standard Bible Encyclopedia*, vol. 2, p. 985.

3. Robert L. Hubbard, Jr., "Israel, Kingdom of," in *The International Standard Bible Encyclopedia*, vol. 2, p. 926.

were three great religious revivals and four periods of spiritual decline. The erratic nature of the nation's faithfulness to the Lord eventually led to her downfall. In 586 B.C., the Babylonians, under the authority of King Nebuchadnezzar, conquered Jerusalem, destroyed Solomon's temple, and ravaged the countryside of Judah (25:1–21, 2 Chron. 36:17–21). Large numbers of people were taken captive and exiled to Babylonia. It was during the final years of Judah's existence that Jeremiah served most of his ministry as a prophet of God.

D. His era. God called Jeremiah to begin his prophetic ministry in the thirteenth year of Josiah's reign (Jer. 1:2). Josiah became king over Judah in 640 B.C. and, in the eighth year of his reign, was converted to the worship of the one true God (2 Chron. 34:1, 3a). During the twelfth year of his rule, Josiah inaugurated religious reform in Judah (vv. 3b–7). It was one year after the initiation of this reform that Jeremiah began his ministry (627 B.C.). But he was not to serve as a prophet in a nation that would remain faithful to God. Following Josiah's death in 609, his son Jehoahaz, or Joahaz, was made king. But he was deposed by the Egyptian monarch Neco II after ruling only three months (36:1–3).[4] Neco II then appointed Jehoahaz's brother Eliakim to govern Judah and changed Eliakim's name to Jehoiakim (v. 4). He ruled eleven years, and he "did evil in the sight of the Lord" before the Babylonian king Nebuchadnezzar seized him and sent him to Babylon in chains (vv. 5b–6). Jehoiakim's son, Jehoiachin, became king and "reigned three months and ten days in Jerusalem," doing "evil in the sight of the Lord" until Nebuchadnezzar exiled him to Babylon and replaced him with Zedekiah (vv. 9–10). Zedekiah governed Judah from 597 to 586. Like many of his predecessors, he also despised the Lord and His spokesmen (vv. 11–16). Consequently, God brought Nebuchadnezzar against him and Judah, thereby bringing about the demise of the southern kingdom (vv. 17–21). During Judah's last years, the priests were unfaithful, the prophets hypocritical, the politicians self-serving—and the Jewish people approved it all (Jer. 5:23–31). Jeremiah, however, stood firmly for the Lord, warning the Judeans of impending doom for their rebellion against God. As he carried out his ministry, Jeremiah saw Judah's decadence grow and witnessed her defeat at the hands of a polytheistic nation. What a frustrating and sorrowful time for a man of God to live and serve in!

---

4. See C. Hassell Bullock, *An Introduction to the Old Testament Prophetic Books* (Chicago: Moody Press, 1986), p. 193.

II. Jeremiah's Appointment and Calling

Perhaps because of the intimidating and wicked times in which Jeremiah was to prophesy, the Lord chose to assure him of his call with words designed to motivate and encourage him.

A. God's confirmation. The Lord first said to Jeremiah, " 'Before I formed you in the womb I knew you, / And before you were born I consecrated you; / I have appointed you a prophet to the nations' " (Jer. 1:5). Jeremiah was shaped, set apart, and chosen by God to serve as a prophet in Judah's declining years. Even his personality, spiritual gifts, and natural abilities were divinely given so that the Lord could use him during this momentous period in Jewish history.

B. Jeremiah's reaction. In spite of what God said, Jeremiah did not immediately accept his call to ministry. With a strong measure of reluctance caused by feelings of inadequacy, Jeremiah objected that he did not have the eloquence or experience necessary for the prophetic task (v. 6). After all, he was only a youth—probably in his late teens or early twenties. Jeremiah was apparently afraid that his youthful inexperience would not warrant the respect he needed to gain a hearing from the Jewish people.

C. God's reconfirmation. The Lord did not allow Jeremiah to remain preoccupied with his own inadequacies and thus shrink back from accepting his appointment as a prophet. God told Jeremiah to disregard his lack of experience and not give in to his fear, because his ministry would be guided and protected every step of the way (vv. 7–8). "Then," Jeremiah recounted, "the Lord stretched out His hand and touched my mouth, and the Lord said to me, 'Behold, I have put My words in your mouth' " (v. 9). To this God added: " 'See, I have appointed you this day over the nations and over the kingdoms, / To pluck up and to break down, / To destroy and to overthrow, / To build and to plant' " (v. 10). Jeremiah was to be God's man amidst perverse nations. And the prophet's message was to be one of rebuke and destruction as well as renewal and construction. Although his ministry would not be popularly accepted, it would be sustained by God's active presence.

Personal Application

First Corinthians 1:26–2:5 confirms what Jeremiah 1 suggests: God's normal practice is to choose those whom man perceives as unlikely candidates to perform the tasks of ministry. In doing so, the Lord discourages His people from being paralyzed by their weaknesses and encourages them

---

4

to depend on Him for the resources they need to accomplish their appointed jobs. Do you feel inadequate to do what God has called you to? Do people put you down or fail to take you seriously because of your inexperience? If so, are you beginning to question your usefulness to the Lord? Take heart! If you are where God wants you, doing His work, keep at it. The Lord will stand by you and reward you for your loyalty to Him.

III. God's Prediction and Jeremiah's Personality

God forewarned Jeremiah about what He was going to do through him. The prophet was told that he would be used to pronounce divine judgment on the Judeans " 'concerning all their wickedness' " (Jer. 1:16a). In addition, the Lord commanded Jeremiah to prepare himself to declare the impending judgment with courage (v. 17). Indeed, God said, " 'I have made you today as a fortified city, and as a pillar of iron and as walls of bronze against the whole land, to the kings of Judah, to its princes, to its priests and to the people of the land' " (v. 18). Did this mean that Jeremiah's message would be readily received? Not at all! As the Lord told Jeremiah, " 'They will fight against you, but they will not overcome you, for I am with you to deliver you' " (v. 19). So for over forty years Jeremiah carried out a ministry that was ignored, ridiculed, and threatened. Did he maintain a sense of joy through it all? Was he always enthusiastic about doing God's work? Again, the answers are negative. As he witnessed Judah constantly spurning his warnings, Jeremiah lapsed into periods of prolonged weeping (9:1, 14:17). At times he questioned the goodness and wisdom of God (14:18–21). And there were occasions when Jeremiah felt that everyone was against him (15:10), including the Lord (20:7–8). He even became so dismayed during his ministry that he cursed the day of his birth and questioned why he had ever been born (vv. 14–18). To top it all off, he had been commanded by God not to marry, which made it difficult for him to find someone to share his burdens with (16:1–2). So Jeremiah—sad, lonely, introspective, unappreciated, even hated—carried on with the prophetic task he had been given. Although he felt like quitting, he refused, with the Lord's help, to give in to that temptation. Notice Jeremiah's words:

> But if I say, "I will not remember Him
> Or speak anymore in His name,"
> Then in my heart it becomes like a burning fire
> Shut up in my bones;
> And I am weary of holding it in,

And I cannot endure it. . . .
But the Lord is with me like a dread champion;
Therefore my persecutors will stumble and not prevail.
They will be utterly ashamed, because they have failed,
With an everlasting disgrace that will not be forgotten.
(20:9–11)

IV. Jeremiah's Example and Our Response

When we feel unsuccessful, discouraged, misunderstood, and ill-treated, we should remember Jeremiah and realize that the Lord does not call all of us to a life filled with human applause and earthly reward. Some of us will have to stand alone and minister unwelcomed and unappreciated. But regardless of the response our work for the Lord receives, we can be reassured in the fact that God is with us, accomplishing His good purpose (Rom. 8:28). For nothing is too difficult for the Creator and Sustainer to accomplish (Jer. 32:17, 27).

🌳 Living Insights

Study One ▆▆▆▆▆▆▆▆▆▆▆▆▆▆▆▆▆▆▆▆▆▆▆▆▆▆▆▆▆▆▆▆▆▆▆

If you've never studied the life of Jeremiah, you may be surprised to see that this prophet of God was such a melancholy man. But there's a lot more to this person, as you'll soon discover!

● Let's do a biographical sketch of the prophet Jeremiah. Make a copy in your notebook of the following chart and begin reading the Book of Jeremiah. As you find phrases that describe Jeremiah's life, jot them down on your chart in the appropriate column. Some examples are provided below to give you an idea of what to look for. We'll continue this discovery in the next study, so bite off a realistic chunk of this book—then go for it.

A Biographical Sketch of Jeremiah			
Strengths	Weaknesses	Positive Circumstances	Negative Circumstances
faithful	*initially insecure*	*appointed by God*	*thrown in the stocks*

●

6

🐢 *Living Insights*

Is Jeremiah starting to become a real person to you? One of the advantages of doing a biographical study is that the character takes on flesh and blood!

● Let's continue looking at the life of Jeremiah. Make a new copy of this chart in your notebook or simply continue using the chart you copied in study one. Then take up where you left off in the Book of Jeremiah.

A Biographical Sketch of Jeremiah			
Strengths	Weaknesses	Positive Circumstances	Negative Circumstances

Jeremiah's Journal
Survey of Lamentations

At one time or another, all of us have enjoyed the fleeting pleasures of sin. Perhaps, while engaged in wicked delights, some of us even considered the potential consequences of our wrongdoing. Chances are, however, that these thoughts were quickly shrugged off or ingeniously rationalized away. Because we are sinners by nature, we are prone to shove aside the anguishing reality of the effects of compromise so that we can more thoroughly embrace the thrills of evil. Realizing this, the Lord has graciously inspired and preserved the Lamentations of Jeremiah, which records the devastating consequences that flowed from Judah's rebellion against God. As we read the pages of this book, we will find ourselves examining our lives and asking ourselves if the bitter fruit of disobedience is worth the tremendous price it exacts. The wages of sin affect not only us but also those we live and work with. As if that were not enough, the Scriptures testify that our disobedience to the Lord can also bring ruin to the neighborhood, city, and country we live in. We must take sin seriously. Jeremiah's journal of lament will help us see this like few other books in God's Word. So let's dig into these ancient memoirs and prepare ourselves to learn from Judah's mistakes.

I. Some Introductory Information

Before taking a survey of Lamentations, it would be good for us to get some introductory information about the book.

A. The title. Originally, Lamentations was untitled. So the Hebrews referred to the book by its first word, *êkâh*, which means "How!" or "Alas!" (Lam. 1:1, 2:1, 4:1). Later in Jewish history, the rabbis called it *qînôt*, "lamentations," which became the book's title in the Talmud—a collection of rabbinical laws and comments on the Mosaic Law—and the Septuagint—the first Greek translation of the Old Testament.[1]

B. The writer. Although the human author never names himself in Lamentations, both Jewish and Christian traditions identify Jeremiah as the book's composer. In fact, the Septuagint added the following as an introduction to the book: "And it came to pass, after Israel was led into captivity and Jerusalem laid waste, that Jeremiah sat weeping and lamented with this lamentation over Jerusalem, and said . . ."[2] Besides this external support for

1. See Walter C. Kaiser, Jr., *A Biblical Approach to Personal Suffering* (Chicago: Moody Press, 1982), p. 30; R. K. Harrison, *Introduction to the Old Testament,* reprint (Grand Rapids, Mich.: William B. Eerdmans Publishing Co., 1979), p. 1065; Charles H. Dyer, "Lamentations," in *The Bible Knowledge Commentary: Old Testament Edition,* edited by John F. Walvoord and Roy B. Zuck (Wheaton, Ill.: Victor Books, 1985), p. 1207.

2. As quoted by Harrison in his *Introduction to the Old Testament,* p. 1069.

Jeremaic authorship, there is a great deal of internal evidence. Bible expositor Charles Dyer summarizes some of the relevant facts in this way:

> Several ideas used by Jeremiah in his prophecy [i.e., the Book of Jeremiah] reappear in Lamentations (cf. Jer. 30:14 with Lam. 1:2; and cf. Jer. 49:12 with Lam. 4:21). In both books the writer said his eyes flowed with tears (Jer. 9:1, 18; Lam. 1:16; 2:11); and in both the writer was an eyewitness of Jerusalem's fall to Babylon and pictured the atrocities that befell Jerusalem in her last days (Jer. 19:9; Lam. 2:20; 4:10).[3]

C. The date. Lamentations describes the desolation of Jerusalem in poetic terms that express deep personal and national anguish. Given this, it is reasonable to assume that the book was composed shortly after Jerusalem was conquered by the Babylonians in the summer of 586 B.C. This would probably place the writing of Lamentations between late 586 and early 585, while Jeremiah was still in war-torn Jerusalem (see Jer. 39:11–14).[4]

D. The historical setting. A study of the circumstances that led up to the writing of Lamentations provides the necessary background for a sound understanding of the book's contents. We know from the Book of Jeremiah that injustice, immorality, and idolatry were rampant in Judah. To illustrate this fact, God told the prophet Jeremiah that if one faithful Hebrew could be found in Jerusalem, the city would be spared from divine retribution (Jer. 5:1). The result of Jeremiah's search foretold Judah's end:

> "An appalling and horrible thing
> Has happened in the land:
> The prophets prophesy falsely,
> And the priests rule on their own authority;
> And My people love it so!
> But what will you do at the end of it?"
> (vv. 30–31)

The answer to this question was that Judah would suffer the consequences of her willful rebellion against God. And what were they? The fruits of her sin began in 588 B.C. when the Babylonian army surrounded Jerusalem and cut off supplies to the city. As Jerusalem stood paralyzed, Babylonian troops

---

3. Dyer, "Lamentations," p. 1207. Added support for Jeremaic authorship of Lamentations can be found in Kaiser's book *Personal Suffering*, pp. 24–29, and in Gleason L. Archer, Jr.'s work *A Survey of Old Testament Introduction,* rev. ed. (Chicago: Moody Press, 1974), pp. 365–67.

4. See Dyer, "Lamentations," pp. 1207–8.

vanquished Egypt—Judah's ally—and, one after another, crushed the other Judean cities. The nineteen-month-long siege of Jerusalem eventually led to social and religious chaos within her walls. As famine began to spread, starving mothers killed and ate their own children (Lam. 2:20a, 4:10). "Idolatry flourished as the people cried out to any and every god for deliverance. Paranoia gripped the people until they were willing to kill God's prophet [Jeremiah] as a traitor and spy just because he spoke the truth."[5] Finally, on July 18, 586 B.C., the walls of Jerusalem were breached, and the Babylonian military poured into the city (2 Kings 25:4a). During the confusion, the Judean monarch Zedekiah and what was left of his army tried to escape. But the Babylonians pursued them and captured the king near Jericho (vv. 4b–5). After Zedekiah was brought before King Nebuchadnezzar, his sons were executed in his presence, his sight was destroyed, and he was chained and ushered off to Babylon (vv. 6–7). Following these events, Nebuchadnezzar went to Jerusalem and supervised the removal of its valuables, the burning of its buildings, the complete destruction of its walls, and the deportation of the majority of the surviving Hebrews to Babylon (vv. 8–17). On top of all this, Nebuchadnezzar had "the [Jewish] princes hung by their hands in public execution"[6] and slaughtered the priests and prophets "in the sanctuary of the Lord" (Lam. 2:20b; cf. 2 Kings 25:18–21, Jer. 39:6). By mid-August of 586 B.C., Jerusalem was "a jumbled heap of smoldering rubble."[7] Jeremiah had witnessed her utter demise (Jer. 39:1–14). Probably while surveying what little was left of the once proud capital of Judah, the prophet sat down and tearfully penned his journal, Lamentations.

II. A Brief Overview of Lamentations

As we study Jeremiah's lament, we will discover that it is composed of five dirges and has a literary structure which brings the message of the book to a climax in chapter 3. A closer examination of this pattern reveals that chapters 1, 2, 4, and 5 each have 22 verses, while chapter 3 has 66 verses. Furthermore, in the first two chapters, each three-line stanza begins with the letter of the Hebrew alphabet that succeeds the one beginning the previous stanza until each of the 22 letters has been utilized. Chapter 3 continues this acrostic pattern, but with a marked literary crescendo. That is, each of the three lines in every stanza occurring in the third chapter "begins with the same

5. Dyer, "Lamentations," p. 1208.

6. Kaiser, *Personal Suffering,* p. 19.

7. Dyer, "Lamentations," p. 1208.

letter of the alphabet and is given separate verse numbers."[8] The fourth chapter indicates a decrescendo in intensity by carrying on the acrostic device with two-line stanzas. Finally, the book closes with a chapter "that is not an acrostic even though it simulates the shape and form of an acrostic in that it has twenty-two verses and resembles certain prayers of corporate lament such as Psalms 44 and 80."[9] Given these details and the context of the book, Lamentations can be visually represented in this way:

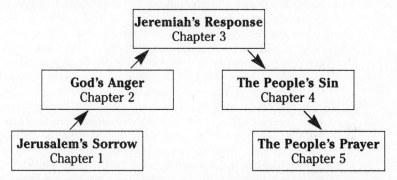

Jeremiah's Response
Chapter 3

God's Anger
Chapter 2

The People's Sin
Chapter 4

Jerusalem's Sorrow
Chapter 1

The People's Prayer
Chapter 5

The layout of Lamentations made it a relatively easy book for the Hebrews to memorize. Apparently, Jeremiah wanted the Jews to always remember the great loss they experienced as a consequence of their sins. But, as Eugene H. Peterson suggests, there was probably another purpose for choosing this structure:

> One of the commonest ways to deal with another's suffering is to make light of it, to gloss it over, to attempt shortcuts through it. Because it is so painful, we try to get to the other side quickly. Lamentations provides a structure to guarantee against that happening. A regular Talmudic idiom speaks of keeping the Torah from aleph to tau or, as we would say, from A to Z. Lamentations puts the idiom to work by being attentive to suffering. It is important to pay attention to everything that God says; but it is also important to pay attention to everything that men and women feel, especially when that feeling is as full of pain and puzzlement as suffering.
>
> The acrostic is a structure for taking suffering seriously. The endless patience for listening to and paying attention to the suffering is emphasized in the fact that not only is Lamentations an acrostic—it *repeats* the

8. Kaiser, *Personal Suffering,* p. 16.
9. Kaiser, *Personal Suffering,* p. 16.

acrostic form. It goes over the story again and again and again and again and again—five times.[10]

With this pattern and these purposes in mind, let's peruse the content of each chapter in Lamentations.

A. Chapter one: The city speaks . . . lonely and groaning. In the first part of this dirge, Jerusalem seems to cry out to Jeremiah in her sorrow, and the prophet faithfully records her lament. It quickly becomes clear that Jerusalem lies in ruin because of her unfaithfulness to God. Notice these poetic descriptions:

> How lonely sits the city / That was full of people! / . . . She weeps bitterly in the night. / . . . She has none to comfort her. / . . . All her pursuers have overtaken her / In the midst of distress. / . . . All her gates are desolate; / Her priests are groaning, / Her virgins are afflicted, / And she herself is bitter. / . . . For the Lord has caused her grief / Because of the multitude of her transgressions; / . . . Jerusalem sinned greatly, / Therefore she has become an unclean thing. (vv. 1–8a)

Through verse 11, Jeremiah acts as the city's spokesman. But in the latter half of chapter 1, Jerusalem speaks for herself. She expresses anguish over being despised by those who travel near her ruins (vv. 11b–12a). She recognizes that God has judged her for her sin, but that does not lessen her pain or relieve her groans (vv. 12b–22).

B. Chapter two: The Lord speaks . . . angry and judging. This chapter reads as if Jeremiah heard God's voice coming from the rubble of Jerusalem and recorded what the Lord said. Consider these words of judgment:

> He has cast from heaven to earth / The glory of Israel. / . . . In fierce anger He has cut off / All the strength of Israel. / . . . In the tent of the daughter of Zion / He has poured out His wrath like fire. / The Lord has become like an enemy. / He has swallowed up Israel; / He has swallowed up all its palaces; / He has destroyed its strongholds / And multiplied in . . . Judah / Mourning and moaning. (vv. 1b–5)

Toward the end of this dirge, we are given a description of what must have been a horrible sight: "On the ground in the streets / Lie young and old, / My virgins and my young men / Have fallen by the sword. / Thou hast slain them in the day of Thine anger, / Thou hast slaughtered, not sparing" (v. 21).

---

10. Eugene H. Peterson, *Five Smooth Stones for Pastoral Work* (Atlanta: John Knox Press, 1980), p. 97.

C. Chapter three: The prophet speaks . . . broken and crying. As if responding to the words of the Lord in chapter 2, Jeremiah says that he shares—even identifies himself with—Judah's pain:

> I am the man who has seen affliction / Because of the rod of His wrath. / . . . He has caused my flesh and my skin to waste away, / He has broken my bones. / He has besieged and encompassed me with bitterness and hardship. / . . . He is to me like a bear lying in wait, / Like a lion in secret places. / He has turned aside my ways and torn me to pieces; / He has made me desolate. (vv. 1–11)

But even in the midst of great suffering and unceasing tears (v. 49), Jeremiah finds hope in God's mercy: "The Lord's lovingkindnesses indeed never cease, / For His compassions never fail. / They are new every morning; / Great is Thy faithfulness. / 'The Lord is my portion,' says my soul, / 'Therefore I have hope in Him.' / The Lord is good to those who wait for Him, / To the person who seeks Him" (vv. 22–25).

D. Chapter four: The possessions speak . . . empty and unsatisfying. The fourth dirge focuses on the insecurity of wealth and the sinfulness of the Jewish people. Apparently, the citizens of Judah had thought that their possessions would protect them from harm. But observe what Jeremiah states:

> How dark the gold has become, / How the pure gold has changed! / . . . The tongue of the infant cleaves / To the roof of its mouth because of thirst; / The little ones ask for bread, / But no one breaks it for them. / Those who ate delicacies / Are desolate in the streets; / Those reared in purple / Embrace ash pits. (vv. 1–5)

So great was the judgment on Judah because of her disobedience to God that "the hands of compassionate women / Boiled their own children; / They became food for them" (v. 10a). Thus Jeremiah could write, "The Lord has accomplished His wrath, / He has poured out His fierce anger; / And He has kindled a fire in Zion / Which has consumed its foundations" (v. 11).

E. Chapter five: The captives speak . . . hungry and hurting. In the final dirge, Jeremiah offers a prayer, standing as a representative of the Jews who survived God's wrath. The captives, as it were, cry out to the Lord, requesting Him to remember their desolate condition and pleading with Him to restore them completely. The thrust of this prayer is found in these verses:

> The joy of our hearts has ceased; / Our dancing has been turned into mourning. / The crown has fallen

from our head;/Woe to us, for we have sinned!/
...Thou, O Lord, dost rule forever;/Thy throne is
from generation to generation./Why dost Thou
forget us forever;/Why dost Thou forsake us so
long?/Restore us to Thee, O Lord, that we may be
restored;/Renew our days as of old,/Unless Thou
hast utterly rejected us,/And art exceedingly angry
with us. (vv. 15–22)

III. Some Relevant Application

In Psalm 137, we read that when the Jewish captives entered Babylon,
they "sat down and wept" (v. 1a). And when they were asked to sing
some of the hymns of their faith, they said, "How can we sing the
Lord's song/In a foreign land?" (v. 4). How tragic are the consequences of sin! Though sin tantalizes us with promises of lasting
happiness and satisfaction, it delivers only fleeting joy and robs us
of all that makes life worth living. Lamentations stands as a potent
reminder to all generations that the path away from God leads to
heartache and destruction, whereas the road to Him brings content-
ment and the fullness of life everlasting. Which path are you trav-
eling? Is it worth the cost?

 Living Insights

Study One ▄▄

In our first lesson we drew a biographical sketch of Jeremiah. In this
study we want to do a survey of Jeremiah's journal—Lamentations.
* Copy the following chart into your notebook; then read Lamentations 1:1–3:38. Look for words or phrases that speak of Jerusalem,
  the Lord, or Jeremiah and list them in the appropriate column. This
  exercise will give you a better understanding of Jeremiah's book.

A Survey of Lamentations 1:1–3:38		
Jerusalem	God	Jeremiah

We are a few verses beyond the halfway point in our survey of Lamentations. Let's finish up our look at this ancient book.

• Reduplicate the following chart or just extend the columns of the chart you used in the previous study. Continue your survey of Lamentations by looking for words or phrases in 3:39–5:22 that refer to Jerusalem, God, or Jeremiah.

A Survey of Lamentations 3:39–5:22		
Jerusalem	God	Jeremiah

None but the Lonely Heart
Lamentations 1

Imagine yourself as a survivor of a long military campaign that destroyed the social and spiritual fabric of your community and burned your city to the ground. While kicking through the rubble in the streets, you stumble across a half-melted mailbox. As you examine it, you finally make out the letters impressed on the metal nameplate. Tears well up in your eyes as you recognize the name as that of your closest friend. "Why?" you cry out, clutching the mailbox in your arms. But no one answers. The ravaged city and the dead who litter her ruins speak only of pain and shattered dreams, not purpose. You hear a starving baby's whimpers being carried along by the wind as it whistles through empty buildings. Looking down a side street, you see a woman sitting on the ground, holding the head of her lifeless husband in her lap, despondently yet lovingly stroking his hair. Lonely . . . hurt . . . broken . . . without hope, you fall to your knees, drop your head to your waiting hands, and sob uncontrollably. That's a semblance of how Jeremiah must have felt as he wandered through the once glorious city of God after it had been left desolate by the idolatrous Babylonian army. Of course, he knew judgment was coming and why. And he faithfully warned the populace to repent of their sins or suffer the consequences. But neither his knowledge of impending destruction nor his obedience to carrying out the prophetic task lessened the deep sorrow he felt as he looked upon the smoldering rubble of Jerusalem. Let's step into his sandals and survey the brokenness with him as he witnesses firsthand the devastating effects of sin.

I. The City Speaks
The first chapter of Lamentations is summarized well by Old Testament scholar Walter Kaiser:

> Jerusalem is personified as a woman who has been forsaken by her friends, massacred by her enemies, left bereft of her former glory, and now stands comfortless and without any "resting place." Zion in her stateless, friendless, hopeless, godless, and Messiahless condition was without a "resting place;" her condition was the reverse situation of the Moabitess, Ruth, who found a place of rest in Jehovah and Judah (Ruth 1:9; 3:1).[1]

With a mixture of humiliation, guilt, grief, and depression, Jerusalem laments over her demise. Let's learn from her as we listen to her expressions of sorrow and regret.

A. Through Jeremiah. Observing the tragic scene around him, Jeremiah takes eleven verses to speak in behalf of the city of

---

1. Walter C. Kaiser, Jr., *A Biblical Approach to Personal Suffering* (Chicago: Moody Press, 1982), p.43.

God. In Lamentations 1:1–7, the prophet focuses on the loneliness of Jerusalem. He describes her as a widow who has suffered tremendous loss. He says that the once greatly populated and highly esteemed city is now void of people and mocked by her enemies (vv. 1, 5b, 6, 7b). Her allies "have become her enemies" and "her adversaries have become her masters" (vv. 2b, 5a). Mourning has replaced happiness; fear has won out over courage (vv. 3, 6b). No one attends her feasts of worship, and she lays desolate and groaning, with no one to comfort her (vv. 3–4). Given this, it is little wonder that Jerusalem is pictured as a widow who "weeps bitterly in the night" (v. 2a). But why has Jerusalem suffered so severely? The answer comes through with honesty and remorse:

> The Lord has caused her grief
> Because of the multitude of her transgressions; ...
> Jerusalem sinned greatly,
> Therefore she has become an unclean thing....
> Her uncleanness was in her skirts;
> She did not consider her future;
> Therefore she has fallen astonishingly. (vv. 5b–9a)

What did the Jews do to warrant such a devastating judgment? The Lord tells us in these words: " 'My people have committed two evils: / They have forsaken Me, / The fountain of living waters, / To hew for themselves cisterns, / Broken cisterns, / That can hold no water' " (Jer. 2:13). Put another way, the Hebrews (1) forsook the Lord and His way and (2) substituted the temporal for the eternal. They became so earthly-minded that they were of no heavenly good. Carnality replaced spirituality; personal pleasure, rather than godly commitment, became their standard for living.

Some Application for Life

Are you facing a fork in the road that requires you to make a decision to walk either with God in the power of His Spirit or with sin in the strength of your flesh? Have you honestly contemplated the consequences of going in the wrong direction? The message that comes from the ruins of Jerusalem is: Don't live for the present without regard for the future; commit yourself to serving God today and forever.

B. On her own. At the end of Lamentations 1:11, Jerusalem starts to speak for herself. The city not only echoes and confirms Jeremiah's observations, but she expresses her agony by describing the extraordinary nature of her pain. The city calls on the Lord to look on her reproach (v. 11b). And she rhetorically asks passersby if they can find anyone who hurts as much as she (v. 12a). After all, her pain was inflicted by the Lord " 'on the day of His fierce anger' " (v. 12b). Jerusalem goes on to describe that awful day:

> "From on high He sent fire into my bones,
> And it prevailed over them;
> He has spread a net for my feet;
> He has turned me back;
> He has made me desolate,
> Faint all day long.
> The yoke of my transgressions is bound;
> By His hand they are knit together;
> They have come upon my neck;
> He has made my strength fail;
> The Lord has given me into the hands
> Of those against whom I am not able to stand.
> The Lord has rejected all my strong men
> In my midst;
> He has called an appointed time against me
> To crush my young men;
> The Lord has trodden as in a wine press
> The virgin daughter of Judah." (vv. 13–15)

Because of this outpouring of divine wrath, Jerusalem is in deep mourning (v. 16a). No one, not even God, can be found to comfort her (v. 16b). Indeed, the Lord is the One who has made sure that the city will find no relief or rest (v. 17). Does this bring complaints of injustice from Jerusalem? No; instead, she upholds the Lord's righteousness and again confesses her rebelliousness (v. 18a). Then, for the first time in Lamentations, the city pours out her pain to God and exhorts Him to judge her adversaries as He has promised (vv. 20–22). This change in Jerusalem's heart shows that God's discipline was accomplishing one of its intended purposes—namely, to bring His people to the place of repentance and of dependence on Him.

II. The Messiah Speaks

Jerusalem's cries express a timeless truth: Only those who have personally experienced the depths of loneliness can understand the anguish of a lonely heart. And no individual, group, or people has ever suffered the pangs of alienation more intensely than has the Son of God, Jesus Christ. For over thirty years, the spotless Lamb walked among sinners and met their needs—only to be betrayed, beaten, mocked, and crucified by those He sought to help. He died alone . . . forsaken by God and despised by man. The prophet Isaiah foretold the Savior's anguish in terms that are reminiscent of Lamentations 1:

> He was despised and forsaken of men,
> A man of sorrows, and acquainted with grief;
> And like one from whom men hide their face,
> He was despised, and we did not esteem Him.
> Surely our griefs He Himself bore,
> And our sorrows He carried;
> Yet we ourselves esteemed Him stricken,
> Smitten of God, and afflicted.
> But He was pierced through for our transgressions,
> He was crushed for our iniquities;
> The chastening for our well-being fell upon Him,
> And by His scourging we are healed.
> All of us like sheep have gone astray,
> Each of us has turned to his own way;
> But the Lord has caused the iniquity of us all
> To fall on Him. (Isa. 53:3–6)

III. Comfort for the Lonely Heart

Are you suffering alone? Is there no one to comfort you or give you rest? Do you feel as if people don't really understand your pain? Jesus knows what you are going through, and He longs to ease your hurt. Listen to His words: " 'Come to Me, all who are weary and heavy-laden, and I will give you rest. Take My yoke upon you, and learn from Me, for I am gentle and humble in heart; and You shall find rest for your souls. For My yoke is easy, and My load is light' " (Matt. 11:28–30). Will you place yourself in His care today?

Living Insights

Study One

Jeremiah is like a newspaper reporter, graphically describing the groanings of Jerusalem. His words are laden with emotions that most of us have felt at some time in our lives. Let's examine more closely what Jeremiah says.

- There is an excellent method of personal Bible study known as *paraphrasing.* It is the rewriting of a Scripture text in your own words. Let's try this exercise with Lamentations 1:1–22. Read through the passage; then paraphrase it. Try to bring out the intensity of the feelings conveyed in the words. It might help if you imagine yourself as a Jewish survivor in a war-ravaged Jerusalem.

Continued on next page

🖋️ *Living Insights*

"None but the lonely heart can feel this anguish." Have you experienced the truth of this statement? Has loneliness marked your past? Is it an ongoing struggle today? How can it be overcome?

- What is your strategy for defeating the enemy of loneliness? Using a blank page in your notebook, write about this subject. Include your thoughts on the following areas:

  —What is it about loneliness that causes such hurt?
  —When are you most susceptible to loneliness?
  —What has helped to bring you out of it in the past?
  —How has the *Lord* helped you in times of loneliness?

My Strategy for Fighting Loneliness

Words from the Woodshed

Lamentations 2

The Lord's desires for His people are summarized in one clear and challenging command: "As obedient children, do not be conformed to the former lusts which were yours in your ignorance, but like the Holy One who called you, be holy yourselves also in all your behavior" (1 Pet. 1:14–15). What happens, however, when Christians choose to go their own way? How does God deal with believers who stubbornly refuse to obey Him? The prophet Hosea provides a poetic answer to these questions: "They sow the wind, / And they reap the whirlwind" (Hos. 8:7a). That is, those who invest themselves in a lifestyle of sin receive as their return the judgment of God. Eliphaz restates this truth with characteristic candor:

"According to what I have seen, those who plow iniquity
And those who sow trouble harvest it.
By the breath of God they perish,
And by the blast of His anger they come to an end."
(Job 4:8–9)

In short, Hosea and Eliphaz are saying *we reap what we sow.* This spiritual principle was strikingly illustrated in the wholesale destruction of Jerusalem—a punishment that fell on the Jews because of their persistent disobedience to God. Lamentations graphically records the consequences of their pursuit of immediate pleasure. The picture we are given is not a pretty one, but it is nonetheless realistic and relevant. So let's heed the Lord's words in Jeremiah's journal of lament.

I. Some Consequences of Disobedience

In Lamentations 2, Jeremiah recounts the measures God took in His discipline of Judah. As he does, he suggests five results of a sinful lifestyle that apply to any individual or community that disobeys God's counsel. Let's examine these consequences and reflect on their pertinence to our lives.

A. Diminishing of one's dignity and unique impact. The prophet exclaims, "How the Lord has covered [or disgraced] the daughter of Zion [i.e., Jerusalem] / With a cloud in His anger! / He has cast from heaven to earth / The glory of Israel" (v. 1a).[1] God has destroyed the homes and strongholds of this once beautiful city, and "He has profaned the kingdom and its princes" (v. 2b). Judah no longer enjoys national prominence; neither do her leaders possess the power and position to guide her destiny. The sins of her people have brought her shame and have removed her godly influence from among the nations.

---

1. Walter Kaiser, Jr. gives linguistic support for understanding the Hebrew term translated *covered with a cloud* to mean "disgraced" in his book *A Biblical Approach to Personal Suffering* (Chicago: Moody Press, 1982), p. 74, fn. 8.

B. Removal of one's stability and vitality. Jeremiah goes
on to say that God's "fierce anger . . . has cut off / All the strength
of Israel" (v. 3a). The Lord has allowed Judah's enemies to be
His instrument of judgment (v. 3b). As a result, His wrath has
consumed the Jews like fire (vv. 3c, 4b). God has torn Judah's
foundation out from under her and "slain all that were pleasant
to the eye" in her capital, Jerusalem (v. 4b).

C. Multiplication of inner anguish. The prophet adds that
amidst Judah's tremendous losses, she has also made some terri-
ble gains. For example, the Lord who was once her Protector
"has become like an enemy" (v. 5a). Thus, "He has swallowed
up Israel . . . [and] all its palaces" (v. 5b). He has even destroyed
all her defenses, leaving her stripped and vulnerable (v. 5b).
No wonder "mourning and moaning" have been greatly multi-
plied in Jerusalem, "the daughter of Judah" (v. 5c). The same
pain that was felt on a national level in Judah is described in
2 Samuel 18 as occurring on a personal plane. In the context of
this passage, King David has been ruling over united Israel and
strengthening her politico-economic foothold in the world. However, it seems that he has neglected his family because of the
great amount of time these tasks have absorbed. In addition,
David has begun to reap the consequences of his adultery with
Bathsheba and his murder of her husband, Uriah (2 Sam. 11:1–12:14).
The king's illegitimate child has died (12:16–23); his son, Amnon,
has raped his own sister, Tamar (13:1–22); David's other son,

Absalom, has avenged Tamar's honor by having Amnon murdered (vv. 24–29); and David has had to flee Jerusalem because of Absalom's attempt to take the throne by force (15:1–18). During the aftermath of these events, Joab, the commander of David's army, decides to kill Absalom as a "favor" to David (18:1–18). Once the deed is complete, Joab sends a messenger to give the "good news" to the king (vv. 19–21). David retreats "to the chamber over the gate and [weeps]" when he receives word about what has happened (v. 33a). While pacing back and forth in the privacy of his room, he cries out repeatedly, " 'O my son Absalom, my son, my son Absalom! Would I had died instead of you, O Absalom, my son, my son!' " (v. 33b). David's decisions to disobey God had caused him to reap a harvest of civil strife and agonizing personal loss.

> **Personal Inventory**
> Have your compromises with sin begun to bring pain into your life? Is your guilt deepening and your anguish intensifying? Are those whom you love suffering because of your failure to walk with God?

D. Feelings of abandonment and emptiness. In Lamentations 2:6–8, Jeremiah describes what God has done to the worship center and walls of Jerusalem:

> He has violently treated His tabernacle . . . ;/He has destroyed His appointed meeting place;/The Lord has caused to be forgotten/The appointed feast and Sabbath . . . ,/And He has despised king and priest./ . . . The Lord has rejected His altar,/He has abandoned His sanctuary;/He has delivered into the hand of the enemy/The walls of her palaces./ . . . The Lord determined to destroy/The wall of the daughter of Zion./ . . . He has not restrained His hand from destroying. (vv. 6–8a)

> **Personal Inventory**
> Has the pleasure promised by sin begun to destroy your happiness, vitality, and spirituality? Are you praying less often and attending church more sporadically? Has your worship become an empty sham? Do you feel abandoned by God and alienated from your friends and family?

E. Heartbreaking absence of vision and purpose.
Jeremiah looks around the ruins of Jerusalem and notices that
"her prophets find / No vision from the Lord" (v. 9b). The elders
of the city are sitting on the ground in silence (v. 10a). "They
have thrown dust on their heads; / They have girded themselves
with sackcloth" (v. 10b). And "the virgins of Jerusalem" have
knelt and "bowed their heads to the ground" (v. 10c). This scene
describes the total humiliation and awful loss of worth felt by
the Jewish survivors. In verses 11 through 16, we find Jeremiah
struggling with how to console the people, but he sadly confesses that neither himself nor any other human being is able
to comfort them. In fact, he tells us that many are finding pleasure
in the Hebrews' pain.

Personal Inventory

Have you lost your godly perspective and sense of purpose
for living? Are you full of shame and misery? Have you
retreated into yourself? Are comforters absent and mockers
abundant?

II. God's Responsibility and Man's Response
Although Lamentations repeatedly affirms that judgment has fallen
on the Jews because of their disobedience to God, it also makes
clear the fact that their punishment has come directly from the Lord
(v. 17). God is the One who has brought this incredible misery upon
them. And the punishment He has inflicted has caused the desired
response from His people—intense sorrow, contrite hearts, broken
wills, and dependent spirits (vv. 18–22).

III. Some Truths to Consider
Too often we rely on God's grace and patience to protect us from
the consequences of our unfaithfulness. But the biblical passages
we have considered in this lesson tell us that the Lord will not allow
His children to hide their sin behind His mercy. Certainly, He will
give them ample opportunities to turn back to Him. But He usually
will not keep them from reaping the wicked harvest they have
planted. Indeed, if His people continue to ignore His warnings, they
will be taken into God's "woodshed" to receive the discipline they
rightfully deserve and desperately need (cf. Heb. 10:26–31, 12:4–13).
At times, of course, it seems as though the righteous are never
rewarded for their faithfulness to the Lord and the wicked are never
punished for their sins (Ps. 73:1–14). But as the psalmist learned so
long ago, this perception is not accurate. Take a few moments to
reflect on his words:

When I pondered to understand this [i.e., the apparent
      prosperity of the wicked],
It was troublesome in my sight
Until I came into the sanctuary of God;
Then I perceived their end.
Surely Thou dost set them in slippery places;
Thou dost cast them down to destruction.
How they are destroyed in a moment!
They are utterly swept away by sudden terrors! . . .
Whom have I in heaven but Thee?
And besides Thee, I desire nothing on earth.
My flesh and my heart may fail,
But God is the strength of my heart and my
      portion forever.
For, behold, those who are far from Thee will perish;
Thou hast destroyed all those who are unfaithful to Thee.
      (vv. 16–27)

Whom will you serve today? The Lord of glory, or the fleeting pleasures of sin? The choice is yours to make, and the consequences yours to bear.

Living Insights

Study One

Lamentations 2 is a reminder of some of the results of sin. In these twenty-two descriptive verses is a message we all need to hear and understand. Let's take this opportunity to gain a deeper knowledge of this passage.

- There are a number of terms in this chapter that can be considered key words. After copying the following chart into your notebook, read through Lamentations 2, and jot down in the left column the words you think are crucial for understanding the chapter. Then, with the help of a good Bible dictionary,[2] write a concise definition of each word. Finally, summarize your thoughts by writing a statement in the right column explaining each term's significance.

Continued on next page

---

2. Some Bible dictionaries we would suggest are these: *Unger's Bible Dictionary*, by Merrill F. Unger, 3d ed., rev. (Chicago: Moody Press, 1966); *Nelson's Illustrated Bible Dictionary* (Nashville: Thomas Nelson Publishers, 1986); and *The Zondervan Pictorial Bible Dictionary* (Grand Rapids, Mich.: Regency Reference Library, Zondervan Publishing House, 1967).

Key Words in Lamentations 2			
Key Words	Verses	Definitions	Significance

 Living Insights

Study Two

Sow the wind, reap the whirlwind. This is a true principle of life. Let's spend some time considering areas of disobedience in our lives that could bring us under the discipline of God.

- Look over the following phrases. Then put a check (√) by any that are currently present in your life.
  ___ Loss of dignity
  ___ Loss of impact
  ___ Instability
  ___ Lack of vitality
  ___ Anguish
  ___ Loneliness
  ___ Lack of vision
  ___ Lack of purpose
- Are any of the experiences you marked consequences of disobedience in your life? Can you think of sins you've committed that may have brought about these negative results?
- Spend some time in prayer, asking for God's help in dealing with these areas.

Infinite Compassion
Lamentations 3:1–32

When we suffer loss, it is only natural for us to grieve. And in our emptiness and sorrow, it is also normal that we focus for a time on ourselves and our misery. However, if our attention continues to be directed inward, we will eventually lose our perspective and our hope. Life will become a confused mixture of "If only I had . . . ," "I remember when . . . ," "If I knew then what I know now . . . ," and "Why . . . ?" Soon guilt, bitterness, self-degradation, and even self-justification will lead to an emotional tailspin that could permanently scar or ruin a life, sometimes tragically ending it in suicide. Where is God in all this? Does He abandon us when we fall on bad times? The late C. S. Lewis felt as if that were so after his wife died of cancer. He expressed his thoughts with disquieting honesty:

> When you are happy, so happy that you have no sense of needing Him, so happy that you are tempted to feel His claims upon you as an interruption, if you remember yourself and turn to Him with gratitude and praise, you will be—or so it feels—welcomed with open arms. But go to Him when your need is desperate, when all other help is vain, and what do you find? A door slammed in your face, and a sound of bolting and double bolting on the inside. After that, silence. You may as well turn away.[1]

How many of us can identify with Lewis's feelings! And yet, we must admit that since God is infinitely good and loving, He will never forsake us, nor will He allow pain to afflict us unless it is in our best interest (Rom. 8:28, Heb. 13:5b–6, James 1:2–4). Even the fires of His discipline are designed to burn away the dross that keeps us from becoming pure images of Jesus Christ (Heb. 12:5–11, 1 Pet. 4:12–19). Truly, His compassion is great! Jeremiah remembered the unfailing love of God while feeling abandoned, oppressed, humiliated, and bitter. What he learned during his darkest hour can provide us with hope and encouragement during our times of distress—even when those periods are due to our own rebellion against God.

I. Broken by Affliction

Jeremiah begins Lamentations 3 with a general statement of the pain he has experienced: "I am the man who has seen affliction / Because of the rod of His wrath" (v. 1). The Hebrew term translated *rod,* which literally means "club," stands for the weapon God used to bring judgment on Judah (cf. Jer. 51:20). In other words, the prophet is saying that he, as an individual and as a representative

---

1. C. S. Lewis, *A Grief Observed* (New York: Seabury Press, 1961), p. 9.

27

of Judah,[2] has witnessed the devastation caused by the Lord's war against His disobedient people. But he has not been simply a casual or sympathetic observer of Judah's affliction. Rather, Jeremiah has personally suffered her torment; he has become a victim of the fallout from divine chastisement. Specifically, the Lord forced him to stumble in the dark instead of guiding him to walk in the light (Lam. 3:2). The prophet has felt "God's hand of favor ... become a fist of adversity"[3] (cf. v. 3). Judgment has brought him anguish, bitterness, and physical misery (vv. 4–5). He has even come to view his situation to be "as hopeless as [that of] those who had died long ago and are now in the grip not only of the grave but even more tragically in the grip of hell"[4] (cf. v. 6, Ps. 88:3–6). Feeling imprisoned and chained (Lam. 3:7), he laments, "When I cry out and call for help, / He shuts out my prayer" (v. 8). He thinks that all avenues of escape have been blocked (v. 9). And wherever he turns, he sees God, like a bear or lion in hiding, waiting to attack and maul him (vv. 10–11). He even feels that the Lord uses him as a target for His arrows (vv. 12–13). As if this were not enough, Jeremiah grieves over the fact that he has been publicly mocked, emotionally embittered, trampled underfoot, deprived of peace, and stripped of happiness (vv. 14–17). Thus, with words of deep discouragement and weariness, Jeremiah summarizes his condition: " 'My strength has perished, / And so has my hope from the Lord' " (v. 18). Looking within and without, the prophet finds only brokenness and dejection.

II. Encouraged with Compassion
From Lamentations 3:19 to the end of the chapter, Jeremiah turns his eyes toward heaven. In doing so, he finds what he and the Jews so desperately need—divine compassion.

A. Humility of soul. The foundation of Jeremiah's prayer is twofold. First, he asks God to remember the pain he has suffered (v. 19). And second, he expresses that his affliction has pushed him to the brink of despair (v. 20). The prophet bows before God bruised, broken, and humbled. There is no pride in him— only remorse and a sense of total dependence on the Lord.

B. Hope in God. Then, in his sunken and vulnerable position, Jeremiah recalls three truths about the nature of God that give

2. Two scholars that provide the evidence for understanding Jeremiah as representing the Jews as well as himself in Lamentations 3 are: Walter C. Kaiser, Jr., in his book *A Biblical Approach to Personal Suffering* (Chicago: Moody Press, 1982), pp. 75–77; and Charles H. Dyer, in his commentary "Lamentations," in *The Bible Knowledge Commentary: Old Testament Edition,* edited by John F. Walvoord and Roy B. Zuck (Wheaton, Ill.: Victor Books, 1985), pp. 1216–17.

3. Dyer, "Lamentations," p. 1217.

4. Kaiser, *A Biblical Approach to Personal Suffering,* p. 84.

him hope and encouragement (v. 21). The first is *God's love never ends* (v. 22a). Jeremiah sees evidence for this truth in the fact that he and all his fellow Jews were not annihilated by the Lord's wrath. The original Hebrew text states this truth in verse 22a, which the New International Version translates accordingly: "Because of the Lord's great love we are not consumed."[5] Bible expositor Charles Dyer brings out the reasoning behind Jeremiah's thought in this passage:

> Judah was down, but not out. God was punishing Judah for her sin, but did not reject her as His covenant people. The word for "great love" is *hesed*, which has the idea of loyal love. God was sticking by the people He had chosen. The covenant made with Israel in Deuteronomy 28 . . . had not been abrogated. In fact God's loyal love could be seen in His faithfulness in carrying out the curses He had promised while at the same time preserving a remnant. The judgment itself was a witness to the fact that God had not abandoned His people.[6]

The second truth Jeremiah recalls is *God's concern never fails* (Lam. 3:22b). In fact, the Lord's expressions of compassion "are new every morning" (v. 23a). The night may seem lonely and bleak, but the dawn of a new day is a reminder that God is still preserving and caring for His people. The third truth Jeremiah finds hope in is this: *God's faithfulness never diminishes* (v. 23b). Regardless of how untrusting and disobedient believers may be, the Lord "remains faithful; for He cannot deny Himself" (2 Tim. 2:13). What a profound assurance of His unlimited grace and trustworthiness! No wonder Jeremiah finally proclaims, " 'The Lord is my portion,' says my soul, / 'Therefore I have hope in Him' " (Lam. 3:24).

III. Strengthened through Rejection

Continuing to concentrate on the character of God, Jeremiah draws out from his reflections some practical suggestions for growing through adversity. *Wait patiently* is the first piece of counsel he gives (v. 25). This is not to be a passive kind of waiting but the kind that involves seeking out God in prayer (v. 25b). In addition, believers should *wait silently* for the Lord to deliver them from suffering and to ultimately restore them (v. 26). This advice does not negate the suggestion to engage in petitionary prayer. However, it does emphasize

---

5. *New International Version of the Holy Bible* (Grand Rapids, Mich.: Zondervan Bible Publishers, 1978).

6. Dyer, "Lamentations," p. 1217.

the need for believers to patiently endure their painful experience and to learn whatever God wishes them to as a result of their trial. Lastly, believers should *submit willingly* to God's providence, even when they are in the throes of adversity (vv. 27–30). Why? Because "the Lord will not reject forever" (v. 31). One day, chastisement will end and restoration will begin. Another reason is that when the Lord "causes grief," He cushions it with the compassion that flows from "His abundant lovingkindness" (v. 32). Granted, His great concern for believers may not always be obvious, but it is nonetheless continually active.

IV. Some Application for Today

Regardless of what we have lost—dignity, integrity, moral purity, finances, employment, health, a loved one—the message of Jeremiah is that we have not been abandoned. The Lord is at our side, faithfully and compassionately meeting our needs. We must rest in this fact before we can find relief. From this biblical truth, however, arises a question we dare not fail to address—namely, If God is always so loving toward us, why does He often seem silent and aloof when we cry out to Him for help? C. S. Lewis answers this question by pointing out that the problem lies with us, not with the Lord:

> You can't see anything properly while your eyes are blurred with tears. You can't, in most things, get what you want if you want it too desperately: anyway, you can't get the best out of it. 'Now! Let's have a real good talk' reduces everyone to silence, 'I *must* get a good sleep tonight' ushers in hours of wakefulness. Delicious drinks are wasted on a really ravenous thirst. Is it similarly the very intensity of the longing that draws the iron curtain, that makes us feel we are staring into a vacuum when we think about our dead? . . .
>
> And so, perhaps, with God. I have gradually been coming to feel that the door is no longer shut and bolted. Was it my own frantic need that slammed it in my face? The time when there is nothing at all in your soul except a cry for help may be just the time when God can't give it: you are like the drowning man who can't be helped because he clutches and grabs. Perhaps your own reiterated cries deafen you to the voice you hoped to hear.[7]

So how can we regain our ability to receive God's love when our sorrow is deep? Jeremiah gives us the answer: Wait patiently . . . wait silently . . . submit willingly.

7. Lewis, *A Grief Observed,* pp. 37–38.

Living Insights

The only way Jeremiah could endure the pain of his circumstance was to recall God's infinite compassion. That's what Lamentations 3 is all about.

- Let's take a look at Lamentations 3:1–32 in a variety of versions. Check your bookshelf for different translations and paraphrases of the Bible. Read this text in the versions you have, paying particular attention to the theme of God's unbounded compassion. In doing this exercise, you'll see how a fresh look at this familiar text will help to bring out new and different insights.

 Living Insights

In an earlier study we learned that Lamentations was written in an acrostic style to aid the Hebrews in memorization. Perhaps Jeremiah had this memory aid in mind when he said, "This I recall to my mind, / Therefore I have hope" (3:21). Let's do some memory work of our own.

- Since Lamentations 3:21–23 marks the turning point of this book, let's concentrate on it. Write out these verses on an index card and read them aloud over and over. You will find that before too long, they will be part of your memory. As a result, you will be able to use them, as Jeremiah did, to find hope in stressful situations.

The Pit
Lamentations 3:33–66

In Hebrews 4, we find these words about the nature, scope, and effectiveness of Scripture: "The word of God is living and active and sharper than any two-edged sword, and piercing as far as the division of soul and spirit, of both joints and marrow, and able to judge the thoughts and intentions of the heart. And there is no creature hidden from His sight, but all things are open and laid bare to the eyes of Him with whom we have to do" (vv. 12–13). As we read Lamentations we certainly experience the truth of these verses. In this Old Testament book the consequences of disobedience are exposed for us to see. And when we look for sin's effects, we discover confusion, sorrow, bitterness, loneliness, despair, pain . . . even death. The picture given is bleak, but it is not one without hope. God stays with His people, no matter how unfaithful they may become. Jeremiah learned this while suffering in the pit of evil's consequences—one which had been dug by the Judean Jews. When he finally looked up from his circumstances, he found God mercifully applying the soothing balm of infinite love to his wounds. The prophet's experience communicates a message that stands as the central theme of Lamentations: *The effects of disobedience are great, but the compassion of the Lord is abundantly greater.* Regardless of how deep a pit we dig for ourselves, God is there, loving us still. In the latter half of Lamentations 3, Jeremiah reaffirms and expands on this climactic message. Let's open ourselves to the truth it conveys and the hope it brings.

I. Truths to Remember

Jeremiah spent about forty years warning the Judean Jews that divine judgment would come unless they chose to repent of their sins and turn back to living God's way. But the prophet's pleas went unheeded. As a consequence, God allowed the Babylonian military to unleash its power on Judah, destroying whatever got in its path. The ruins that were left behind stood as a stark reminder of the devastation that continued defiance can bring. While surveying the rubble of Jerusalem, Jeremiah laments over the city and its people. In the midst of his tears, he remembers that the Lord's love never ceases, His compassion never fails, and His faithfulness never diminishes (Lam. 3:22–23). These truths gave him the assurance he needed to endure tremendous suffering and overcome deep despair (v. 24).

II. Theology to Live By

As he continues to focus his thoughts on the Lord, Jeremiah recalls three more facets of His divine nature which provide comfort when days are bleak.

A. God is just. This truth is conveyed in these words:

> For He does not afflict willingly,
> Or grieve the sons of men.
> To crush under His feet
> All the prisoners of the land,
> To deprive a man of justice
> In the presence of the Most High,
> To defraud a man in his lawsuit—
> Of these things the Lord does not approve.
> (vv. 33–36)

The Lord is not a cosmic sadist or a heavenly brute. Certainly He disciplines us, but not because He derives any degree of cruel delight in watching us suffer. The Lord's goal is to give us what is best for us, whether we want it or not. He loves us too much to do less. The writer of Hebrews expresses this fact well:

> It is for discipline that you endure; God deals with you as with sons; for what son is there whom his father does not discipline?... Furthermore, we had earthly fathers to discipline us, and we respected them; shall we not much rather be subject to the Father of spirits, and live? For they disciplined us for a short time as seemed best to them, but He disciplines us for our good, that we may share His holiness. All discipline for the moment seems not to be joyful, but sorrowful; yet to those who have been trained by it, afterwards it yields the peaceful fruit of righteousness. (Heb. 12:7–11)

B. God is sovereign. Next, Jeremiah fixes his attention on the authority God has over all creation. The prophet observes that only the Lord can accurately declare what will be (Lam. 3:37). If He says something will take place, it will. He cannot make mistakes, nor can anything thwart His hand or nullify His plan (cf. Job 42:2, Ps. 33:6–11, Isa. 46:9–10). In addition, "both good and ill go forth" from the Lord (Lam. 3:38). This passage does not mean that God is the cause of evil. Scripture reveals that the Lord cannot even approve wickedness, much less cause it (Hab. 1:13a; cf. James 1:13–17). However, this verse in Lamentations does teach that both prosperity and adversity ultimately come from the Lord. Sometimes He will directly cause them to occur, but other times He will permit secondary agents to carry out His bidding—for example, when God allowed the Babylonian army to conquer Judah as punishment for her sins. Of course, whether the Lord is the direct or indirect cause of good and ill in a particular situation is an issue that is sometimes difficult to resolve from our limited perspective. But we can be

33

sure of one thing: The Lord is always in sovereign control of whatever transpires in the universe. Job's acceptance of this fact gave him the ability to handle the tremendous loss of his children, possessions, and health. It even brought him the strength to withstand his wife's pleas to curse God and die (Job 2:9). Job's response to his wife is instructive: " 'You speak as one of the foolish women speaks. Shall we indeed accept good from God and not accept adversity?' " (v. 10). The obvious answer is, "Certainly not, since both prosperity and adversity are designed for our ultimate benefit" (cf. Rom. 8:28).

C. God is holy. The Lord is not only just and sovereign but also holy. He is set apart from His creation as its morally pure Creator, Sustainer, Redeemer, and Judge. Man, on the other hand, is wicked and unjust, deserving only of God's wrath. Therefore, Jeremiah asks, "Why should any living mortal, or any man, / Offer complaint in view of his sins?" (Lam. 3:39). Any affliction human beings suffer for their wrongdoing is well deserved. If they do not wish to experience the fiery judgment of God, they need to examine their lifestyles and repent of their sins (v. 40). However, if individuals choose to persist in their rebellion, the Lord will not pardon them (v. 42). Indeed, He will pursue them with anger and ignore their prayers for relief (vv. 43–44).

III. Pain in the Pit

The Judean Jews learned the hard way that God will not tolerate sin—especially if it comes from believers. Rather than experiencing the joys of obedience, they tried to accrue pleasure through disobedience. As a result, they suffered great loss and intense pain. They were humiliated before the Gentile nations, mocked by their enemies, stricken by panic, and left physically and emotionally desolate (vv. 45–47). Witnessing this awful state of affairs, Jeremiah lowers his head and grieves:

> My eyes run down with streams of water
> Because of the destruction of the daughter of my people.
> My eyes pour down unceasingly,
> Without stopping,
> Until the Lord looks down
> And sees from heaven.
> My eyes bring pain to my soul
> Because of all the daughters of my city.
> My enemies without cause
> Hunted me down like a bird;
> They have silenced me in the pit
> And have placed a stone on me.
> Waters flowed over my head;
> I said, "I am cut off!" (vv. 48–54)

Misery . . . rejection . . . loneliness—these are the fruits of sin. Jeremiah felt them all, even though he was not to blame for the destruction that befell Judah. The wickedness of his fellow countrymen had brought it on him, themselves, and their nation.

IV. Petition from the Pit

Once again, Jeremiah looks up from his tears and lifts his voice to God, seeking the help and consolation only He can give.

A. Jeremiah's requests. From "the lowest pit" the prophet cries out for divine help (vv. 55–56). He exhorts the Lord to judge his case, observe how his enemies mock him, and defend him against his assailants (vv. 59b–63).

B. God's answers. Interwoven with Jeremiah's specific petitions are the Lord's specific answers. God heard Jeremiah's prayer and made His presence known to the prophet (vv. 56a, 57a). The Lord told him not to be afraid; then He defended Jeremiah's cause and saved him from his enemies (v. 58). Indeed, God promised Jeremiah He would repay his enemies by causing their downfall (vv. 64–66). And this the Lord did by bringing about the progressive deterioration of the Babylonian Empire, which led to its overthrow by Cyrus the Persian in 539 B.C.[1]

V. Principles to Observe

There is much in Lamentations 3:33–66 that can help us as we experience times of suffering—especially when the distress of those days is due to the consequences of sin. Let's take note of three principles that emerge clearly from this text.

A. When we find ourselves in "the pit," we need to examine our lives and return to God. The Lord will not respond to our prayers for relief as long as we continue trafficking in sin. However, once we repent of the rebellion that separates us from Him, "He is faithful and righteous to forgive us our sins and to cleanse us from all unrighteousness" (1 John 1:9).

B. When we come across others who are in "the pit," we should seek to comfort them. People who are down need to know that someone cares about them. Giving a helping hand, a listening ear, or a sympathetic embrace will go a long way toward lessening someone else's hurt.

C. Regardless of the adversity we suffer, a sound understanding of God will help ease our pain and provide us with hope. Without a clear grasp on theology—who God

---

1. The collapse of the Babylonian Empire is described in the study guide titled *Daniel: God's Pattern for the Future,* edited by Bill Watkins, from the Bible-teaching ministry of Charles R. Swindoll (Fullerton, Calif.: Insight for Living, 1986), pp. 44–48.

is and how He relates to us—we are adrift on the sea of life, unprepared for the storms that are sure to strike us. However, the better we know God, the more equipped we are to weather whatever comes our way.[2]

![icon] Living Insights

Study One ▬▬▬▬▬▬▬▬▬▬▬▬▬▬▬▬▬▬▬▬▬▬▬▬▬▬▬

What holds life together during times of despair? A correct understanding of God, that's what! Jeremiah focused on three divine attributes which gave him the proper perspective on personal suffering. Let's examine each one in greater depth.

- The following chart lists several references that relate to God's justice, sovereignty, and holiness. As you discern what each verse teaches concerning the nature of God, summarize your conclusions on a copy of this chart. Turn this study into an opportunity to get to know the Lord more fully.

Three Attributes of God
Justice
2 Chronicles 19:7
Job 4:17
Psalm 19:9
Psalm 89:14
Isaiah 45:21
Sovereignty
1 Samuel 2:6–8
1 Chronicles 29:11–12
Matthew 6:13
Romans 9:1–33
Holiness
Leviticus 19:2
1 Samuel 2:2
Psalm 47:8
Isaiah 6:3
Isaiah 57:15
1 John 1:5

2. At the end of this study guide, the section titled "Books for Probing Further" lists some helpful materials that focus on the doctrine of God and other subjects touched on in this series.

A proper understanding of God brings needed and reassuring perspective to life's pain. This truth is too good to pass over quickly. Allow the following questions to serve as either discussion starters or guides for private reflection. Strive for honesty and vulnerability in your answers.

—How does God's justice bring perspective to my pain?

—How does God's sovereignty help me deal with adversity?

—How does God's holiness enlighten my view of suffering?

—What other divine attributes can give me hope while I'm in "the pit"?

—Am I making my situation better or worse by the way I'm responding to it?

—How does Lamentations 3:40 help me find needed relief?

—What else can I draw from this lesson that can provide the resources I need to cope with my crisis?

When the Bottom Drops Out
Lamentations 4, Isaiah 43

What happens when the bottom drops out—when we experience such calamities as great financial loss, an unwanted divorce, the death of a loved one, or intense personal suffering? A teenager named Elie Wiesel lost his faith in God during his calamity—imprisonment at Buna, a Nazi concentration camp. One of the events that drove him to unbelief was the execution of a little boy. Along with thousands of other prisoners, Wiesel was forced to watch members of Hitler's Secret Service lead two men and a child to the gallows for hanging. Once the sentence was carried out, the prisoners were required to march past the execution sight. Wiesel describes in moving terms what he saw and how he felt:

> The two adults were no longer alive. Their tongues hung swollen, blue-tinged. But the third rope was still moving; being so light, the child was still alive....
>
> For more than half an hour he stayed there, struggling between life and death, dying in slow agony under our eyes. And we had to look him full in the face. He was still alive when I passed in front of him. His tongue was still red, his eyes were not yet glazed.
>
> Behind me, I heard [a] man asking: "Where is God now?"
>
> And I heard a voice within me answer him: "Where is He? Here He is—He is hanging here on this gallows...."[1]

Not everyone responded to the horror of the Holocaust as Wiesel did. In fact, numerous survivors of the concentration camps found hope to endure and a deeper meaning to life as a result of their strong religious and moral convictions.[2] Many of them saw God proving that He was alive—caring for their needs, purifying their characters, and judging their captors. So what *does* happen to us when our lives are turned upside down? How *can* we view these times so that we will grow in faith and find the strength to persevere? The Book of Isaiah and The Lamentations of Jeremiah hold the answers. Let's turn to their pages and consider what they reveal.

I. The Feelings

When catastrophe strikes us, there are three feelings we commonly experience. One is *fear*—an incredible sense of panic that frequently overpowers our ability to think clearly and act decisively. Another debilitating emotion is *insecurity*. We become anxious and apprehensive, feeling incapable of coping with the situation. Then, there is *loneliness*—that awful sense of abandonment which leads us to

---

1. Elie Wiesel, as quoted by Philip Yancey in *Open Windows* (Westchester, Ill.: Crossway Books, 1982), pp. 18–19.

2. See Yancey, *Open Windows,* chap. 1.

believe that no one can or even wants to help us. These emotions are not new. Godly men and women have felt them throughout history. In the Book of Isaiah, the Lord even prophesied that the nation of Israel would experience these emotions when she came under His discipline. Thus, He gave Israel counsel to help her endure the coming judgment. First, He said the Jews could counteract their fear and insecurity by realizing that they were His possession—redeemed and cared for by Him (Isa. 43:1). Second, God promised them they could overcome their feelings of loneliness by recalling that He was with them, protecting them:

"When you pass through the waters, I will be with you;
And through the rivers, they will not overflow you.
When you walk through the fire, you will not be scorched,
Nor will the flame burn you." (v. 2)

God acknowledged that the Jews would suffer, but He reassured them that they would not pass through difficult days alone.

II. The Catastrophe

Between 588 and 586 B.C., Judah experienced her darkest hour. Jerusalem—the apple of God's eye—was besieged by the Babylonian army. Cutting off all supplies to the city, the Babylonians set the stage for the capital's demise. Eventually, a great famine swept Jerusalem, and many people died of starvation. When the city finally fell to the invaders, most of those inhabitants who were still alive were exiled to pagan soil to spend the remainder of their days in captivity. The prophet Jeremiah forewarned the Judean Jews of this impending disaster, but he was ignored. Rather than repenting of their sins and turning back to God, the Hebrews persisted in their rebellion and reaped the horrible consequences of their defiance. Lamentations 4 records in poetic form what happened during the siege and subsequent destruction of Jerusalem. The snapshot it gives is unpleasant, but it provides a stark reminder of the awful effects of sin.

A. Some specifics. Reflecting on what he saw among Jerusalem's ruins, Jeremiah exclaims:

How dark the gold has become,
How the pure gold has changed!
The sacred stones are poured out
At the corner of every street.
The precious sons of Zion,
Weighed against fine gold,
How they are regarded as earthen jars,
The work of a potter's hands! (Lam. 4:1–2)

The precious wealth of the city is tarnished and strewn along the streets like unwanted litter. And the people of the city, though worth much more than gold, are treated like valueless clay pots. Furthermore, the Jewish adults have become like cruel animals, refusing to care for the needs of the children (vv. 3–4). Mothers have even begun to kill, boil, and eat their own children (v. 10). Those who were rich and important have been stripped of their wealth and dignity (v. 5). The once handsome and healthy civic leaders are now wandering the streets, barely recognizable because of their blackened and shriveled bodies which are racked by hunger (vv. 8–9).

B. Some characteristics. Intertwined with Jeremiah's descriptions of what happened to Jerusalem are five aspects of virtually any catastrophe.

    1. **Unexpected turmoil.** By Jeremiah's day, Jerusalem had been so thoroughly fortified that even foreign kings considered it to be impregnable (v. 12). Therefore, the Jews who lived within its walls felt safe and secure. They believed that the destruction Jeremiah had predicted could not take place. And yet, to their surprise, Jeremiah's prophecies came true. Jerusalem was not only conquered—it was burned to the ground.

    2. **Overwhelming circumstances.** The prophets and priests who were to act as God's spokesmen in Judah had become corrupt and shed innocent blood (v. 13). The downfall of Jerusalem, however, abbreviated their sin-ridden "ministries." Now they wandered as blind men in the streets, crying out for no one to touch them since their wickedness had so polluted them (vv. 14–15a). Indeed, people were treating these former religious leaders as lepers, forcing them out of their communities and into the heathen nations that disdained them (vv. 15b–16). This must have made the priests and prophets feel helpless, alienated, and unable to cope.

    3. **Absence of comfort.** When Jerusalem was surrounded by the Babylonians, the Jewish people looked to other nations—especially to Egypt—for help. But no one came to their aid. Indeed, no country *could* save them (v. 17). They were beyond human help or comfort. Only God could rescue them, but He would not do so because He was punishing them for their wickedness.

    4. **Inescapable situations.** Realizing that they could not hang their hopes on outside aid, the Jews tried to escape the stranglehold of the Babylonian army themselves. But their enemies relentlessly pursued and slaughtered them (vv. 18a–19). Unable to escape, they became despondent (v. 18b).

    5. **Involuntary exposure.** The tragedy that befell the Jews uncovered their iniquities. The same would eventually occur

to Edom—a nation that actively promoted and rejoiced over Jerusalem's demise (vv. 21–22).

III. The Lessons

"It is a terrifying thing to fall into the hands of the living God" (Heb. 10:31). Lamentations makes this abundantly clear. However, there are valuable lessons we can learn while suffering—whether or not our affliction is the result of prior personal sin. From our study in Isaiah 43 and Lamentations 4, at least two lessons can be drawn.

A. Sudden devastation is often the beginning of a process of reconstruction. The Lord does not build on impure or weak foundations. Whatever He cannot purify, He destroys and rebuilds. Either process can be intensely painful; each can even appear to be brutal and unmerciful. But these are the only ways we can receive His best and thereby become truly happy. C. S. Lewis states this truth well:

> We were made not primarily that we may love God (though we were made for that too) but that God may love us, that we may become objects in which the Divine love may rest "well pleased." To ask that God's love should be content with us as we are is to ask that God should cease to be God: because He is what He is, His love must, in the nature of things, be impeded and repelled by certain stains in our present character, and because He already loves us He must labour to make us lovable. We cannot even wish, in our better moments, that He could reconcile Himself to our present impurities—no more than the beggar maid could wish that King Cophetua should be content with her rags and dirt, or a dog, once having learned to love man, could wish that man were such as to tolerate in his house the snapping, verminous, polluting creature of the wild pack. What we would here and now call our "happiness" is not the end God chiefly has in view: but when we are such as He can love without impediment, we shall in fact be happy.[3]

B. Behind the pain of human calamity is the faithful presence of God. The Lord may seem distant—even uncaring—when the bottom drops out of our lives. But if we are members of His forever family, we cannot be abandoned by Him. We have His promise on that: " 'I will never desert you, nor will I ever forsake you' " (Heb. 13:5b). Moreover, as believers, we can

---

3. C. S. Lewis, *The Problem of Pain* (New York: Macmillan Publishing Co., 1962), p. 48.

find comfort in the fact that we cannot be separated from His infinite love. Nothing can take us away from the Lord. Once we are His, we are His forever. God reveals this encouraging truth through these words of the Apostle Paul:

> Who shall separate us from the love of Christ? Shall tribulation, or distress, or persecution, or famine, or nakedness, or peril, or sword?... But in all these things we overwhelmingly conquer through Him who loved us. For I am convinced that neither death, nor life, nor angels, nor principalities, nor things present, nor things to come, nor powers, nor height, nor depth, nor any other created thing, shall be able to separate us from the love of God, which is in Christ Jesus our Lord. (Rom. 8:35–39)

 Living Insights

Study One

One of the finest portraits of God's activity in human tragedy is the story of Job. Have you read it recently? This might be a good time to reconsider what he learned about God and himself through the suffering he endured.

- Read through the Book of Job, looking for references both to God's sovereignty and to Job's suffering. Record your findings on a copy of the following chart. If you're pressed for time, you might want to read just the first six chapters and the last five.

Job: When the Bottom Drops Out

God's Sovereignty		Job's Suffering	
Observations	Verses	Observations	Verses

📖 *Living Insights*

Behind the pain of human calamity is the faithful presence of God. He is at work, caring for needs and rebuilding shattered lives. Let's pause to talk with the Lord about His work of reconstruction in our lives.

- Tell God what's on your heart. Has the bottom dropped out? Are you in the pit? Is the Lord dealing with your disobedience? Have you thanked Him for His infinite compassion? In prayer, share your hurts with God, and then turn your attention to His faithfulness—praise Him!

The Wages of Sin
Lamentations 5

At different times in our history, different cities have been the focal point of a radiating American spirit. In the late eighteenth century, for example, Boston was the center of a political radicalism that ignited a shot heard round the world.... In the mid-nineteenth century, New York became the symbol of the idea of a melting-pot America.... In the early twentieth century, Chicago, city of big shoulders and heavy winds, came to symbolize the industrial energy and dynamism of America....

Today, we must look to the city of Las Vegas, Nevada, as a metaphor of our national character and aspiration, its symbol a thirty-foot high cardboard picture of a slot machine and a chorus girl. For Las Vegas is a city entirely devoted to the idea of entertainment, and as such proclaims the spirit of a culture in which all public discourse increasingly takes the form of entertainment. Our politics, religion, news, athletics, education and commerce have been transformed into congenial adjuncts of show business, largely without protest or even much popular notice. The result is that *we are a people on the verge of amusing ourselves to death.*[1]

Neil Postman is right. Western society *is* consumed with the pursuit of pleasure. From practically every corridor of our culture, advice streams forth, encouraging us to make immediate happiness our ultimate goal. To accommodate this counsel, more sources of entertainment have been provided for us than for any other civilization in human history. With so much time and energy being invested in our achievement of earthly joy, one would think that we would be thoroughly content by now. But if that were true, "we would be telling one another frequently of our unparalleled bliss, rather than trading tranquilizer prescriptions."[2] The fact is that we show all the signs of a people who are receiving the wages of sin: we see increases in drug addiction, alcoholism, mental illness, child abuse, divorce, rape, suicide, and murder. The hard evidence shows that our quality of life is not getting better but becoming worse. As obvious as this seems, our faith in finding happiness apart from God stands undaunted. Rather than facing reality, we continue to pursue a dream that is showing itself to be a nightmare. We desperately need to listen to Jeremiah's laments, for they are a timeless warning that what sin promises, it can never deliver. Only God can bring us the lasting satisfaction we all desire. So let's open our eyes and

1. Neil Postman, *Amusing Ourselves to Death: Public Discourse in the Age of Show Business* (New York: Viking Penguin, 1985), pp. 3–4, emphasis added.

2. John Gardner, *Self-renewal* (New York: W. W. Norton and Co., 1981), as quoted by Tim Hansel in *When I Relax I Feel Guilty* (Elgin, Ill.: David C. Cook Publishing Co., 1979), p. 109.

hearts to what He wants to teach us through the final chapter of Lamentations.

I. O Lord, Remember

The fifth chapter of Lamentations records the prayer of Judah's survivors. Humiliated and brokenhearted, the Jews turn their tear-stained faces heavenward and plead with God to remember their plight (vv. 1–18).

A. What happened. The Hebrews recount the tragedy they have experienced:

> Our inheritance has been turned over to strangers,
> Our houses to aliens.
> We have become orphans without a father,
> Our mothers are like widows.
> We have to pay for our drinking water,
> Our wood comes to us at a price.
> Our pursuers are at our necks;
> We are worn out, there is no rest for us.
> We have submitted to Egypt and Assyria to get
>   enough bread. (vv. 2–6)

B. Why it occurred. The Jews admit that their horrible situation was their punishment for persisting in a sinful lifestyle. Notice their confession:

> Our fathers sinned, and are no more;
> It is we who have borne their iniquities. (v. 7)
> The crown has fallen from our head;
> Woe to us, for we have sinned!
> Because of this our heart is faint;
> Because of these things our eyes are dim.
> (vv. 16–17)

The Hebrew survivors realize that they have learned the art of deceit from their ancestors. But rather than rejecting what they had been taught, they willingly embraced it and committed sins that were worse than those of their forefathers (cf. Jer. 3:25, 16:12). Finally, in their broken condition, the Hebrews stop rationalizing their sin and take full responsibility for their disobedience.

A Discussion on Responsibility

The practice of "passing the buck" has been with us since the time of Adam and Eve. After the first sin in the Garden of Eden, God asked Adam what he had done (Gen. 3:11). Instead of accepting responsibility for his own action, Adam blamed both the Lord and Eve for his transgression (v. 12). Eve responded in a similar way, accusing the serpent for her disobedience (v. 13). Another excellent example of self-justification and rationalization comes from the life of the

---

first Israelite king, Saul. Through the prophet Samuel, the Lord commanded Saul to kill all the Amalekites and to " ' "utterly destroy" ' " all of their possessions (1 Sam. 15:1–3). Saul, however, spared Agag, the king of the Amalekites, and saved "the best of the sheep, the oxen, the fatlings, the lambs, and all that was good" (vv. 8–9). After God revealed to Samuel what Saul had done (vv. 10–11), the prophet went out to the battlefield to meet Saul (v. 12a). When the Israelite king saw him, he greeted him with the claim that God's command had been obeyed (v. 13). "But Samuel said, 'What then is this bleating of the sheep in my ears, and the lowing of the oxen which I hear?' " (v. 14). Realizing he had been caught in his sin, Saul tried to cover his tracks by making his troops out to be the transgressors (v. 15). But Samuel would not allow the monarch to pass the buck. He reminded Saul of what the Lord had told him to do (v. 18); then he asked the king, " 'Why then did you not obey the voice of the Lord, but rushed upon the spoil and did what was evil in the sight of the Lord?' " (v. 19). Determined to exonerate himself, Saul again claimed that he had carried out God's command (v. 20). And he added that his troops had spared the best of the Amalekites' possessions so that they could be sacrificed to God (v. 21). But Samuel saw through Saul's defense and toppled it with these words of denunciation: " 'Behold, to obey is better than sacrifice. / . . . For rebellion is as the sin of divination, / And insubordination is as iniquity and idolatry. / Because you have rejected the word of the Lord, / He has also rejected you from being king' " (vv. 22b–23). Finally, Saul said what he should have said in the beginning: " 'I have sinned; I have indeed transgressed the command of the Lord and your words, because I feared the people and listened to their voice' " (v. 24). To disobey God is a grave matter. But to try to justify our sin or blame someone else for it only compounds the seriousness of our evil. We should accept responsibility for our own actions. In doing so, we will please the Lord and more readily receive His forgiveness.

C. Who it affected. The surviving victims of Judah's desolation lament that the Babylonians had appointed cruel taskmasters to rule over them (Lam. 5:8). The Jews also mention that they were risking their lives just to get bread to eat (v. 9), but that they were unable to get enough to stave off their burning hunger (vv. 9–10). They ache over the fact that the Babylonian invaders assaulted their women, executed their princes, demeaned their elders, and forced their young men to perform the heavy work animals once did (vv. 11–13). It was obvious that sin did not bring the Hebrews what they had been striving for—happiness. Instead, it robbed them of joy and turned their dancing into mourning (v. 15).

II. O Lord, Rule

After calling on God to remember the catastrophe that had befallen them, the Jews exalt His everlasting authority over all creation: "Thou, O Lord, dost rule forever; / Thy throne is from generation to generation" (v. 19). Their knowledge of God's sovereignty then prompts them to ask why the Lord has abandoned them for so long (v. 20). They feel as if God has rejected them because of their sin, and this causes them to wonder whether or not He will leave them in their present state of suffering.

III. O Lord, Restore and Renew

Falling on the mercy of God, the Jewish captives close their prayer by requesting the Lord to forgive their rebellion and restore them to Himself (v. 21a). To this they add their plea for God to renew them to their former glory (v. 21b; cf. v. 16), unless He has totally rejected them (v. 22)—an action they must have realized was impossible, given God's loving character and His promise that He would never abandon them (cf. 3:22–23, 31; Jer. 31:31–40).

IV. Hope for Modern Captives

When we are suffering the consequences of our sin, we frequently feel as the Jews did—abandoned by God and beyond any usefulness to Him. The good news, however, is that the Lord will not—indeed, cannot—forsake those who have placed their faith in Him. In fact, His desire is to restore His people, not reject them. And His goal is to use them in His work, not ignore them. Are you a member of His family who is receiving the wages of wrongdoing? If so, confess your sin and turn back to the Lord. Like the father of the prodigal son, He is waiting to forgive and renew you (Luke 15:11–32).

📖 Living Insights

Study One ▬▬▬▬▬▬▬▬▬▬▬▬▬▬▬▬▬▬▬▬▬▬▬▬▬▬▬▬▬▬

Lamentations is a powerful little book! It has taught us a lot about the Lord, ourselves, and sin. Let's review some of the great truths we have learned together.

• After copying the following chart into your notebook, go back through your Bible, notebook, and study guide. Write out the most *meaningful truth* you gleaned from each lesson. It may have been a main point or a small statement made in passing. Whatever the case, it should be something that was especially significant to you.

The Lamentations of Jeremiah	
Lesson Titles	Meaningful Truths
The Prophet Who Cried a Lot	
Jeremiah's Journal	
None but the Lonely Heart	
Words from the Woodshed	
Infinite Compassion	
The Pit	
When the Bottom Drops Out	
The Wages of Sin	

📖 Living Insights

Study Two ▬▬▬▬▬▬▬▬▬▬▬▬▬▬▬▬▬▬▬▬▬▬▬▬▬▬▬

In the previous Living Insights we reviewed the meaningful truths we discovered during our study of Lamentations. Now let's review the *personal applications* we put into action as a result of this study.

- How did Lamentations change your life? Turn back the pages of your study guide, notebook, and Bible in order to refresh your memory about the changes you made. Then, on a copy of the following chart, jot down one application per lesson that made a significant impact on you.

The Lamentations of Jeremiah	
Lesson Titles	Important Applications
The Prophet Who Cried a Lot	
Jeremiah's Journal	
None but the Lonely Heart	
Words from the Woodshed	
Infinite Compassion	
The Pit	
When the Bottom Drops Out	
The Wages of Sin	

Books for Probing Further

In his book *Amusing Ourselves to Death,* Neil Postman makes some observations about the futuristic visions of George Orwell and Aldous Huxley that are all too pertinent to our study of Lamentations:

What Orwell feared were those who would ban books. What Huxley feared was that there would be no reason to ban a book, for there would be no one who wanted to read one. Orwell feared those who would deprive us of information. Huxley feared those who would give us so much that we would be reduced to passivity and egoism. Orwell feared that the truth would be concealed from us. Huxley feared the truth would be drowned in a sea of irrelevance. Orwell feared we would become a captive culture. Huxley feared we would become a trivial culture, preoccupied with some equivalent of the feelies, the orgy porgy, and the centrifugal bumblepuppy. As Huxley remarked in *Brave New World Revisited,* the civil libertarians and rationalists who are ever on the alert to oppose tyranny "failed to take into account man's almost infinite appetite for distractions." In *1984,* Huxley added, people are controlled by inflicting pain. In *Brave New World,* they are controlled by inflicting pleasure. In short, Orwell feared that what we hate will ruin us. Huxley feared that what we love will ruin us.[1]

The Judean Jews of the sixth century B.C. were enamored with "the passing pleasures of sin" (Heb. 11:25b)—a love affair that ended in personal and national desolation. Today, we are repeating their mistake. We are allowing the pursuit of immediate pleasure to turn us away from God and toward ruin. Fortunately, we still have time to change our ways, and we can begin doing so by applying the counsel God has given us through Lamentations. Some of the subjects we covered in our study may have sparked your interest. If you wish to delve into them further, you should find the materials listed in this bibliography especially helpful. But do not use these sources simply as means to stretch your mind; instead, utilize them as aids to draw you closer to the Lord and to make you more effective in the world for Him.

I. Learning about God

Bavinck, Herman. *The Doctrine of God.* Translated, edited, and outlined by William Hendriksen. Grand Rapids, Mich.: Baker Book House, 1977.

Baxter, J. Sidlow. *Majesty: The God You Should Know.* San Bernardino, Calif.: Here's Life Publishers, 1984.

Charnock, Stephen. *The Existence and Attributes of God.* 2 vols. Grand Rapids, Mich.: Baker Book House, 1979.

France, R. T. *The Living God.* Downers Grove, Ill.: InterVarsity Press, 1970.

Hocking, David L. *The Nature of God in Plain Language.* Waco, Tex.: Word Books, 1984.

Lewis, C. S. *Mere Christianity.* Rev. ed. New York: Macmillan Publishing Co., 1952.

Nystrom, Carolyn. *Who Is God?* Illustrated by Wayne A. Hanna. Children's Bible Basics. Chicago: Moody Press, 1980.

Packer, J. I. *Knowing God.* Downers Grove, Ill.: InterVarsity Press, 1973.

Shedd, William G. T. *Dogmatic Theology.* Vol. 1. Reprint. Minneapolis: Klock and Klock Christian Publishers, 1979.

Strauss, Richard L. *The Joy of Knowing God.* Neptune, N. J.: Loizeaux Brothers, 1984.

Thiessen, Henry Clarence. *Lectures in Systematic Theology.* Revised by Vernon D. Doerksen. Grand Rapids, Mich.: William B. Eerdmans Publishing Co., 1979.

Tozer, A. W. *The Knowledge of the Holy.* San Francisco: Harper and Row, 1961.

1. Neil Postman, *Amusing Ourselves to Death: Public Discourse in the Age of Show Business* (New York: Viking Penguin, 1985), pp. vii–viii.

II. Confronting Social Evil

Alcorn, Randy C. *Christians in the Wake of the Sexual Revolution: Recovering Our Sexual Sanity.* A Critical Concern Book. Portland: Multnomah Press, 1985.

Anderson, J. Kerby. *Genetic Engineering.* Grand Rapids, Mich.: Zondervan Publishing House, 1982.

Beals, Art. *Beyond Hunger: A Biblical Mandate for Social Responsibility.* With Larry Libby. A Critical Concern Book. Portland: Multnomah Press, 1985.

Burtchaell, James T. *Rachel Weeping: The Case against Abortion.* San Francisco: Harper and Row, 1982.

Buzzard, Lynn. *With Liberty and Justice.* Wheaton, Ill.: Victor Books, 1984.

Davis, John Jefferson. *Abortion and the Christian: What Every Believer Should Know.* Phillipsburg, N. J.: Presbyterian and Reformed Publishing Co., 1984.

Fowler, Richard A., and House, H. Wayne. *The Christian Confronts His Culture.* Chicago: Moody Press, 1983.

Geisler, Norman L. *Ethics: Alternatives and Issues.* Foreword by Harold B. Kuhn. Grand Rapids, Mich.: Zondervan Publishing House, 1971.

Henry, Carl F. H. *The Christian Mindset in a Secular Society: Promoting Evangelical Renewal and National Righteousness.* A Critical Concern Book. Portland: Multnomah Press, 1984.

Hinchliff, Peter. *Holiness and Politics.* Grand Rapids, Mich.: William B. Eerdmans Publishing Co., 1982.

Kreeft, Peter. *The Unaborted Socrates.* Downers Grove, Ill.: InterVarsity Press, 1983.

Lutzer, Erwin W. *Exploding the Myths That Could Destroy America.* Foreword by John Warwick Montgomery. Chicago: Moody Press, 1986.

Monsma, Stephen W. *Pursuing Justice in a Sinful World.* Grand Rapids, Mich.: William B. Eerdmans Publishing Co., 1984.

Postman, Neil. *Amusing Ourselves to Death: Public Discourse in the Age of Show Business.* New York: Viking Penguin, 1985.

Schlossberg, Herbert. *Idols for Destruction: Christian Faith and Its Confrontation with American Society.* Nashville: Thomas Nelson Publishers, 1983.

Sproul, R. C. *Lifeviews: Understanding the Ideas That Shape Society Today.* A Crucial Questions Book. Old Tappan, N. J.: Fleming H. Revell Co., 1986.

Stott, John. *Involvement: Being a Responsible Christian in a Non-Christian Society.* Vol. 1. A Crucial Questions Book. Old Tappan, N. J.: Fleming H. Revell Co., 1985.

————. *Involvement: Social and Sexual Relationships in the Modern World.* Vol. 2. A Crucial Questions Book. Old Tappan, N. J.: Fleming H. Revell Co., 1985.

Whitehead, John W. *The Separation Illusion: A Lawyer Examines the First Amendment.* Foreword by R. J. Rushdoony. Milford, Ill.: Mott Media, 1977.

III. Resisting Temptation

Busséll, Harold L. *Lord, I Can Resist Anything but Temptation.* Grand Rapids, Mich.: Pyranee Books, Zondervan Publishing House, 1985.

Carroll, Frances L. *Temptation: How Christians Can Deal with It.* Englewood Cliffs, N. J.: Prentice-Hall, 1984.

Cerling, Charles, Jr. *Freedom from Bad Habits.* Foreword by Dwight Harvey Small. San Bernardino, Calif.: Here's Life Publishers, 1984.

Kehl, D. G. *Control Yourself! Practicing the Art of Self-discipline.* Grand Rapids, Mich.: Zondervan Publishing House, 1982.

Lutzer, Erwin W. *How to Say No to a Stubborn Habit—Even When You Feel Like Saying Yes.* Foreword by Stuart Briscoe. Wheaton, Ill.: Victor Books, 1979.

————. *Living with Your Passions.* Foreword by Josh McDowell. Wheaton, Ill.: Victor Books, 1983.

Owen, John. *Sin and Temptation.* Edited and abridged by James M. Houston. Introduction by J. I. Packer. Portland: Multnomah Press, 1983.

Petersen, J. Allan. *The Myth of the Greener Grass.* Wheaton, Ill.: Tyndale House Publishers, 1983.

Swindoll, Charles R. *Moral Purity.* Fullerton, Calif.: Insight for Living, 1985.

————. *Sensuality: Resisting the Lure of Lust.* Portland: Multnomah Press, 1981.

Walters, Richard P. *Jealousy, Envy, Lust: The Weeds of Greed.* Grand Rapids, Mich.: Pyranee Books, Zondervan Publishing House, 1985.

Wilson, Earl D. *Sexual Sanity: Breaking Free from Uncontrolled Habits.* Downers Grove, Ill.: InterVarsity Press, 1984.

IV. Coping with Catastrophe

Baker, Don. *Pain's Hidden Purpose: Finding Perspective in the Midst of Suffering.* Portland: Multnomah Press, 1984.

Bayly, Joseph. *The Last Thing We Talk About.* Rev. ed. Elgin, Ill.: David C. Cook Publishing Co., 1973.

Clarkson, Margaret. *Grace Grows Best in Winter.* Foreword by Joni Eareckson Tada. Grand Rapids, Mich.: William B. Eerdmans Publishing Co., 1984.

D'Arcy, Paula. *Where the Wind Begins.* Wheaton, Ill.: Harold Shaw Publishers, 1984.

Ford, Leighton. *Sandy: A Heart for God.* Downers Grove, Ill.: InterVarsity Press, 1985.

Graham, Billy. *Till Armageddon: A Perspective on Suffering.* Waco, Tex.: Word Books, 1981.

Hansel, Tim. *You Gotta Keep Dancin'.* Elgin, Ill.: David C. Cook Publishing Co., 1985.

Kaiser, Walter C., Jr. *A Biblical Approach to Personal Suffering.* Chicago: Moody Press, 1982.

Koop, Ruth, M.D. *When Someone You Love Is Dying: A Handbook for Counselors and Those Who Care.* With Stephen Sorenson. Grand Rapids, Mich.: Ministry Resources Library, Zondervan Publishing House, 1980.

Lewis, C. S. *A Grief Observed.* New York: Seabury Press, 1961.

————. *The Problem of Pain.* New York: Macmillan Publishing Co., 1962.

Manning, Doug. *Comforting Those Who Grieve: A Guide for Helping Others.* San Francisco: Harper and Row, 1985.

Means, James E. *A Tearful Celebration.* Portland: Multnomah Press, 1985.

Richards, Larry, and Johnson, Paul. *Death and the Caring Community: Ministering to the Terminally Ill.* A Critical Concern Book. Portland: Multnomah Press, 1980.

Schaeffer, Edith. *Affliction.* Old Tappan, N. J.: Fleming H. Revell Co., 1978.

Strauss, Lehman. *In God's Waiting Room: Learning through Suffering.* Chicago: Moody Press, 1985.

Swindoll, Charles R. *When Your Comfort Zone Gets the Squeeze.* Fullerton, Calif.: Insight for Living, 1985.

————. *For Those Who Hurt.* Portland: Multnomah Press, 1977.

Vanauken, Sheldon. *A Severe Mercy.* New York: Bantam Books, 1977.

Vredevelt, Pam W. *Empty Arms.* Portland: Multnomah Press, 1984.

Wiersbe, Warren W. *Why Us? When Bad Things Happen to God's People.* Old Tappan, N. J.: Fleming H. Revell Co., 1984.

Wise, Robert L. *When There Is No Miracle.* Foreword by Rosalind Rinker. Ventura, Calif.: Regal Books, 1977.

Yancey, Philip. *Helping the Hurting.* Portland: Multnomah Press, 1984.

————. *Where Is God When It Hurts?* Grand Rapids, Mich.: Zondervan Publishing House; Wheaton, Ill.: Campus Life Books, 1977.

Acknowledgments

Insight for Living is grateful for permission to quote from the following sources:

Dehoney, Wayne. *An Evangelical's Guidebook to the Holy Land.* Nashville: Broadman Press, 1974. All rights reserved.

Dyer, Charles H. "Lamentations." In *The Bible Knowledge Commentary: Old Testament Edition.* Edited by John F. Walvoord and Roy B. Zuck. Wheaton, Ill.: Victor Books, 1985.

Kaiser, Walter C., Jr. *A Biblical Approach to Personal Suffering.* Chicago: Moody Bible Institute of Chicago, Moody Press, 1982.

Lewis, C. S. *The Problem of Pain.* New York: Macmillan Publishing Co., 1962.

Peterson, Eugene H. *Five Smooth Stones for Pastoral Work.* Atlanta: John Knox Press, 1980.

Postman, Neil. *Amusing Ourselves to Death: Public Discourse in the Age of Show Business.* New York: Viking Penguin, 1985.

Insight for Living
Cassette Tapes
THE LAMENTATIONS OF JEREMIAH

Contained in these eight lessons is a rare and rich verse-by-verse study of one of the lesser-known books of the Bible—The Lamentations of Jeremiah. But how its words are needed today! In this brief journal, the prophet describes his beloved city in ruins and his own people in grief—all because of sin. "Whatever we sow, we reap" pulsates through these serious, soul-searching messages designed to warn the reader against disobeying the voice of God.

			U.S.	Canadian
LAM	CS	Cassette series—includes album cover	$23.75	$30.00
		Individual cassettes—include messages		
		A and B	5.00	6.35

These prices are effective as of June 1986 and are subject to change without notice.

LAM 1-A: *The Prophet Who Cried a Lot*
Jeremiah 1:1–10, 16–19
   B: *Jeremiah's Journal*
Survey of Lamentations

LAM 2-A: *None but the Lonely Heart*
Lamentations 1
   B: *Words from the Woodshed*
Lamentations 2

LAM 3-A: *Infinite Compassion*
Lamentations 3:1–32
   B: *The Pit*
Lamentations 3:33–66

LAM 4-A: *When the Bottom Drops Out*
Lamentations 4, Isaiah 43
   B: *The Wages of Sin*
Lamentations 5

Ordering Information

U.S. ordering information: You are welcome to use our toll-free number (for Visa and MasterCard orders only) between the hours of 8:30 A.M. and 4:00 P.M., Pacific time, Monday through Friday. The number is **(800) 772-8888.** This number may be used anywhere in the continental United States excluding California, Hawaii, and Alaska. Orders from those areas are handled through our Sales Department at **(714) 870-9161.** We are unable to accept collect calls.

Your order will be processed promptly. We ask that you allow four to six weeks for delivery by fourth-class mail. If you wish your order to be shipped first-class, please add 10 percent of the total order cost (not including California sales tax) for shipping and handling.

Canadian ordering information: Your order will be processed promptly. We ask that you allow approximately four weeks for delivery by first-class mail to the U.S./Canadian border. All orders will be shipped from our office in Fullerton, California. For our listeners in British Columbia, a 7 percent sales tax must be added to the total of all tape orders (not including first-class postage). For further information, please contact our office at **(604) 272-5811.**

Payment options: We accept personal checks, money orders, Visa, and MasterCard in payment for materials ordered. Unfortunately, we are unable to offer invoicing or COD orders. If the amount of your check or money order is less than the amount of your purchase, your check will be returned so that you may place your order again with the correct amount. All orders must be paid in full before shipment can be made.

Returned checks: There is a $10 charge for any returned check (regardless of the amount of your order) to cover processing and invoicing.

Guarantee: Our tapes are guaranteed for ninety days against faulty performance or breakage due to a defect in the tape. For best results, please be sure your tape recorder is in good operating condition and is cleaned regularly.

Mail your order to one of the following addresses:

Insight for Living	Insight for Living Ministries
Sales Department	Post Office Box 2510
Post Office Box 4444	Vancouver, BC
Fullerton, CA 92634	Canada V6B 3W7

Quantity discounts and gift certificates are available upon request.

Overseas ordering information is provided on the reverse side of the order form.

Order Form

Please send me the following cassette tapes:
The current series: ☐ LAM CS The Lamentations of Jeremiah
Individual cassettes: ☐ LAM 1   ☐ LAM 2   ☐ LAM 3   ☐ LAM 4

I am enclosing:

$_____   To purchase the cassette series for $23.75 (in Canada $30.00*) which includes the album cover

$_____   To purchase individual tapes at $5.00 each (in Canada $6.35*)

$_____   Total of purchases

$_____   California residents please add 6 percent sales tax

$_____   U.S. residents please add 10 percent for first-class shipping and handling if desired

$_____   *British Columbia residents please add 7 percent sales tax

$_____   Canadian residents please add 6 percent for postage

$_____   **Overseas residents please add appropriate postage** (See postage chart under "Overseas Ordering Information.")

$_____   As a gift to the Insight for Living radio ministry for which a tax-deductible receipt will be issued

$_____   **Total amount due (Please do not send cash.)**

Form of payment:
☐ Check or money order made payable to Insight for Living
☐ Credit card (Visa or MasterCard only)
If there is a balance: ☐ apply it as a donation   ☐ please refund

---

Credit card purchases:
☐ Visa   ☐ MasterCard number _____
Expiration date _____
Signature _____
We cannot process your credit card purchase without your signature.

Name _____
Address _____
_____
City _____
State/Province _____ Zip/Postal code _____
Country _____
Telephone (_____) _____ Radio Station ___ ___ ___ ___

Should questions arise concerning your order, we may need to contact you.

Overseas Ordering Information

If you do not live in the United States or Canada, please note the following information. This will ensure efficient processing of your request.

Estimated time of delivery: We ask that you allow approximately twelve to sixteen weeks for delivery by surface mail. If you would like your order sent airmail, the length of delivery may be reduced. All orders will be shipped from our office in Fullerton, California.

Payment options: Due to fluctuating currency rates, we can accept only personal checks made payable in U.S. funds, international money orders, Visa, and MasterCard in payment for materials ordered. If the amount of your check or money order is less than the amount of your purchase, your check will be returned so that you may place your order again with the correct amount. All orders must be paid in full before shipment can be made.

Returned checks: There is a $10 charge for any returned check (regardless of the amount of your order) to cover processing and invoicing.

Postage and handling: Please add to the amount of purchase the basic postage cost for the service you desire. All orders must include postage based on the chart below.

Purchase Amount		Surface Postage	Airmail Postage
From	To	Percentage of Order	Percentage of Order
$ .01	$15.00	40%	75%
15.01	75.00	25%	45%
75.01	or more	15%	40%

Guarantee: Our tapes are guaranteed for ninety days against faulty performance or breakage due to a defect in the tape. For best results, please be sure your tape recorder is in good operating condition and is cleaned regularly.

Mail your order or inquiry to the following address:

Insight for Living
Sales Department
Post Office Box 4444
Fullerton, CA 92634

Quantity discounts and gift certificates are available upon request.